Co-published in 2011 by:

Helion & Company Limited
26 Willow Road
Solihull
West Midlands
B91 1UE
England
Tel. 0121 705 3393
Fax 0121 711 4075
email: info@helion.co.uk
website: www.helion.co.uk

and

30° South Publishers (Pty) Ltd.
16 Ivy Road
Pinetown 3610
South Africa
email: info@30degreessouth.co.za
website: www.30degreessouth.co.za

Designed & typeset by 30° South Publishers (Pty) Ltd., South Africa
Cover design by 30° South Publishers (Pty) Ltd., South Africa
Printed by Henry Ling Limited, Dorchester, Dorset, UK
ISBN 978-1-907677-39-7

British Library Cataloguing-in-Publication Data
A catalogue record for this book is available from the British Library

A note on the photographs
Most of the colour photographs in this book were taken with an Olympus OM1, 35mm single lens reflex camera. The lenses used were a 50mm Olympus f1.2, a 70 – 220 Soligor f2.4 zoom lens with macro. The film used was Kodak 400ASA colour print film, with the exception of the first spool of Agfa 50ASA colour transparency film. The monochrome shots were taken with an SADF-issue Kodak 35mm SLR camera and SADF-issue b&w film of unknown speed.

The cover photograph of the author under canopy over Cassinga was taken by Sergeant Des Steenkamp, a member of A Company in the attack group.

CONTENTS

GLOSSARY

AFB	airforce base
ANC	African National Congress
Bde	Brigade
Bn	Battalion
Coy	Company
DTA	Democratic Turnhalle Alliance
DZ	drop zone
EW	electronic warfare
FAPLA	*Forças Armadas Populares para a Libertação de Angola* (Popular Armed Forces for the Liberation of Angola)
FNLA	*Frente Nacional para a Libertação de Angola* (National Front for the Liberation of Angola)
HAA	Helicopter Administration Area
HE	high exposive
HQ	headquarters
intrep	intelligence report
JARIC	Joint Air Reconnaissance Intelligence Centre
LZ	landing zone
MAOT	Mobile Air Operations Team
MK	*Umkhonto we Sizwe* (Spear of the Nation), the armed wing of the ANC
MP	Military Police
MPLA	*Movimento Popular para a Libertaçao de Angola* (Popular Movement for the Liberation of Angola)
NATO	North Atlantic Treaty Organization
NSM	national serviceman
Pl	Platoon
PLAN	People's Liberation Army of Namibia, SWAPO's armed wing
POW	prisoner of war
PWC	personal weapons container
RAP	Regimental Aid Post
RPG	rocket-propelled grenade
SAAF	South African Air Force
SADF	South African Defence Force (pre-1994)
SANDF	South African National Defence Force (post 1994)
SWAPO	South West Africa People's Organization
TRC	Truth and Reconciliation Commission
UN	United Nations
UNHCR	United Nations High Commission for Refugees
UNICEF	United Nations Children's Fund.
UNITA	*União Nacional para a Independência Total de Angola* (National Union for the Total Independence of Angola)

INTRODUCTION

Exactly 33 years have passed since the battle of Cassinga. This has enabled all sides in the conflict to view it, and its outcomes, with a certain dispassionate perspective. This is a soldier's story from a military historian's viewpoint. It is an insight into the battle itself, from 'the sharp end', and demonstrates once and for all who was really in command of the offensive. It debunks the idea that Cassinga was a refugee camp and analyzes, for the first time, why it has been so important for SWAPO to maintain that façade for so long. Lastly, it is a paean to combatants on both sides, both living and dead.

The main players were the South West Africa People's Organization (SWAPO); their armed wing, the People's Liberation Army of Namibia (PLAN); the South African Defence Force (SADF); the Cuban military training and advisory cadres and, to a lesser extent, the Angolan army, *Forças Armadas Populares de Libertação de Angola* (FAPLA) and, on the fringes, South Africa's African National Congress's (ANC) armed wing, Umkhonto we Sizwe (MK).

The controversy over the battle still rages, with each anniversary commemorated in Namibia with a public holiday called Kassinga Day and in South Africa, 4 May, Cassinga Day. In South Africa it is commemorated both as a great feat of arms and as a remembrance day for all paratroopers who lost their lives during the long bush war. Most anniversaries are accompanied by the press and media reliving the battle and its many controversies. The various sides cannot even reach agreement as to how to spell the name of what was an old Portuguese local government centre. The Namibians spell it with a 'K' and everyone else with a 'C', as in Cassinga. This book will use the 'Cassinga' spelling because that is how it was spelt on the marker in the centre of the town, and also on the large distance marker on the road leading to the town. The author presumes that the Portuguese know the correct spelling, because they named the town in the first place.

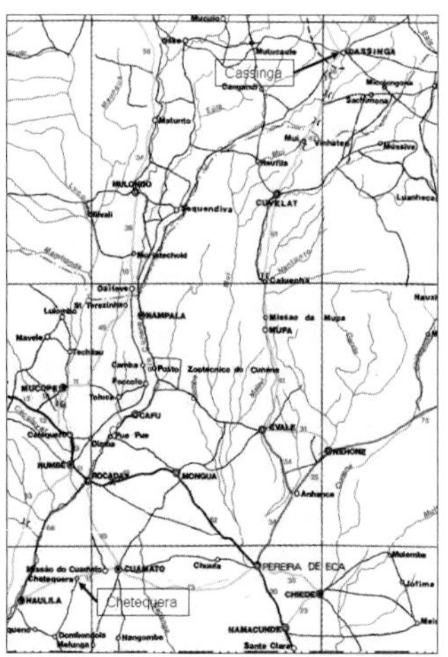

Another talking point, in South Africa at least, was who was in command of the attacking force. Brigadier du Plessis claimed at one time to have been the commander, but everyone else, including SWAPO, knows that Colonel Jan Breytenbach was the commander on the day. The author attended the orders group and all orders were personally hand written, circulated and presented by Colonel Breytenbach.

The South African Truth and Reconciliation Commission Volume 2,

An aerial photograph of Cassinga.

Town marker.

Sam Nujoma.
Source: Wikicommons

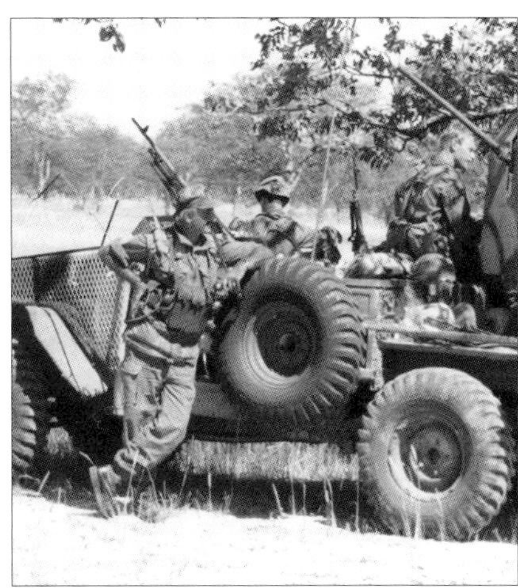

Col Jan Breytenbach at left.
Source: Pathfinder Company

Chapter 2, 'The State Outside South Africa between 1960 and 1990' states: "General Ian Gleeson (101 Task Force), Colonel 'Blackie' de Swardt (SAAF) and Colonel 'Giep' Booysen (SA Medical Services) were in overall command of the actual operation and responsible for its planning. Fighting forces on the ground at Kassinga were led by Colonel Jan Breytenbach (32 Battalion), and Commandant Deon Ferreira, and at Chetequera by Major Frank Bestbier."

Whether Cassinga was a refugee camp or a military base has always been a bone of contention. There was even a Master's thesis written by a former paratroop officer which was sympathetic to the notion that a massacre of refugees took place. Although this officer was not present at the battle, he considerably enhanced his career under an ANC government by his adoption of the party line. The sentiments in the thesis, therefore, could possibly be regarded as expedient and self-serving. The evidence presented in this book and in Colonel Jan Breytenbach's book, *Eagle Strike*, taken together with SWAPO's own photographic record on their website and the photographs the author took at the battle, prove conclusively that Cassinga, code-named 'Moscow' by SWAPO, was a large and well-defended military base. To this day, more than 30 years later, SWAPO still steadfastly refuses to admit that Cassinga was the main military base for their organization in southern Angola. They still insist that it was only a refugee camp, despite the overwhelming evidence, both photographic and archival, to the contrary. SWAPO's own website features photographs of many armed combatants at Cassinga, both male and female, in and out of uniform. This has meant that the exceptionally brave conduct of the SWAPO/PLAN soldiers has never been recognized by their own people; rather, they have been depicted as cowering refugees instead of the brave and resourceful fighters they really were.

The South African Truth and Reconciliation Commission (TRC), a body not kindly disposed toward the SADF, found not one shred of evidence that there was a massacre of civilians or refugees at Cassinga, or that the paratroopers had in any way breached the standard rules of engagement in the execution of their task. However, the TRC did find that the raid was an infringement on the sovereignty of Angola and that the use by the South African Air Force of cluster bombs was contrary to United Nations codes of practice, where unexploded ordnance could harm innocent people long after a battle. These were the only negative aspects the TRC could find, despite Cassinga being one of the most eagerly anticipated 'atrocity' investigations during the lengthy TRC process.

Soldiers and families from all sides today still question the reason why their friends and loved ones died fighting the 'bush war' and at Cassinga in particular. The only answer which makes any sense all these years later is that the conflict allowed Namibia (formerly South West Africa, or SWA) to join the nations of the world as an equal partner. The leader of SWAPO, Sam Nujoma, vowed that he and his organization would take Namibia/South West Africa through the barrel of the gun. For many years SWAPO was not interested in either a negotiated settlement or democratic elections. Their clear objective was to seize power by force and run the country as a communist dictatorship. It was only through a series of setbacks, such as the destruction of his military headquarters at Cassinga, that Nujoma was finally forced to negotiate a settlement and subject the country to democratic processes. Thus Namibia became a democracy. This in turn had an impact on the political evolution in South Africa.

Both liberation movements, SWAPO and its southern neighbour, the ANC/MK, found that, although they could happily foment and maintain unrest, they were never going to win an outright military victory. Both movements lost their major sponsor, the USSR, when the Berlin Wall crumbled. The fact that the government of the day in South Africa outlasted the Soviet Union enabled both Namibia and South Africa to evolve as genuine democracies rather than communist dictatorships. One only has to look at what happened in Zimbabwe to see the result of a communist-backed liberation movement having unrestricted power. The chances are that both Namibia and South Africa would have sunk into rapid ruin had the USSR still been the powerful force that it was prior to 1989.

CHAPTER ONE: BACKGROUND TO THE BATTLE

During the 'Scramble for Africa', which effectively began in 1885, the European powers began grabbing chunks of Africa for themselves. The Germans took South West Africa and in 1886 demarcated the northern border with the agreement of Portugal, who had centuries before claimed Angola as their own.

This foreign ownership proved a harsh experience for the natives of South West Africa. The Germans, after a short honeymoon period posing as protectors of the indigenous population, began a systematic policy of genocide against the Herero and Nama peoples who formed the bulk of the sparsely populated territory. After spirited resistance, both tribes were crushed and South West Africa became a rigidly controlled German colony. This unhappy situation remained the status quo until the outbreak of the First World War.

In 1915, a year after war broke out, the South African government, despite much resistance from German sympathizers in the ruling party's ranks, agreed on a joint allied attack on South West Africa. The Union government forces under Louis Botha led the attack with the Royal Navy helping secure victory by taking the port of Luderitz, cutting off German resupply. The Germans, heavily outnumbered, surrendered to the South Africans in July 1915. Thus ended 31 years of German rule of the territory.

Although General Jan Smuts, a South African member of the British War Cabinet, intended South West Africa to become part of South Africa after the war, he was forced to agree to a compromise. This saw South Africa given a mandate to govern South West Africa. In 1920, this was ratified by the League of Nations, the precursor to the United Nations. South African rule did not bring all that the indigenous people of South West Africa were hoping for. Instead of widespread land restitution, the remaining German settlers were not dispossessed and large numbers of Afrikaners from South Africa, as well as from Angola, were granted large tracts of land which they farmed successfully, largely due to generous grants from the South African government. Until 1948, the territory was governed by an administrator who devolved power downward through a traditional tribal chieftainship system. The country was split into white areas where the German and Afrikaner settler-farmers lived, and the black areas under the tribal chiefs. The franchise was restricted to whites only. The Owamboland region was exclusively black and, where the Herero and Nama people lived within white areas, they were allocated reserves.

In 1922, South Africa came under scrutiny from the League of Nations Mandate Commission when the new Administrator-General, G.R. Hofmeyr, brutally put down a rebellion of Bondelswarts tribesmen who'd refused to pay a new dog tax. Twenty-two years later the United Nations began pressurizing South Africa to submit its mandate to United Nations trusteeship. However, Jan Smuts made a determined effort to incorporate the territory into South Africa, getting the tribal chiefs to petition the United Nations to grant incorporation. With looming Indian independence dominating all else, the United Nations refused to allow this. When the Smuts government was defeated in the 1948 election, the new Nationalist government under Dr D.F. Malan halted the reporting procedure to the UN as the mandate had by then lapsed. The Nationalists then manoeuvred, by creating new parliamentary seats, to effectively incorporate South West Africa as a fifth province into the Union of South Africa, all without UN approval. The UN challenged South Africa's actions in the International Court of Justice, with the court opining that South Africa's mandate should be extended, but that South Africa should resume reporting on South West Africa to the UN Mandate Committee. The South African government rejected this and so began the first of a long stream of resolutions against South African policy.

Meanwhile, indigenous resistance to South African rule was personified by the formation of several small political parties such as the South West African National Union and more notably a consolidation of the Owamboland political party, the Owamboland People's Organization (OPO) into the South West Africa People's Organization (SWAPO). With the help of local and London-based white sympathizers, as well as the Soviets, SWAPO began training recruits in guerrilla warfare.

The South African Police were responsible for the security of the territory until 1973 when the South African Defence Force took over the task. In 1966, the first armed SWAPO incursion took place in South West Africa at Ongulumbashe. It was put down instantly by a combined South African Defence Force and police team.

One of the South African paratroopers who took part in the action was a man who would become SWAPO's nemesis at the battle of Cassinga 12 years later. This man would also become South Africa's most decorated soldier and founder of the three most respected units in the South African Defence Force: the Reconnaissance Commando, 44 Parachute Brigade and 32 Battalion. The soldier was Jan Dirk Breytenbach.

The action at Ongulumbashe also saw the crude beginnings of what was to become a deadly southern African specialty, the Fire Force. Fire Force operations developed from the simple air transport by helicopter of troops and the subsequent encirclement and destruction of the enemy into sophisticated aerial choreography using gunships, troop carriers, fixed-wing aircraft and at times paratroops to vertically envelop and destroy the enemy.

After the first blood had gone to the SADF, SWAPO was forced

D.F. Malan.
Photo: Wikicommons

General Louis Botha.
Photo: Wikicommons

Jan Smuts.
Photo: Wikicommons

Jonas Savimbi.
Photo: Wikicommons

to base itself in distant Zambia as it became untenable to operate from its home territory, Owamboland. However, SWAPO only sporadically infiltrated South West Africa from Zambia. Small teams of guerrillas undertook terrorist acts against white farmers as well as black traditional leaders. Their primary *modus operandi* was to make rapid incursions into the hinterland, lay landmines and then exfiltrate the country, but not before intimidating the local population by means of random murder and political indoctrination.

Compared to their African National Congress (ANC) counterparts, the Umkhonto we Sizwe guerrillas, SWAPO soldiers were of a high calibre: well trained, well disciplined and very fit. South African troops found it difficult to track down an enemy whose flight was often aided by Soviet-supplied amphetamines and well fuelled with Swedish herrings and Dutch chocolate. SWAPO's anti-tracking skills as well as their local knowledge of the land made them an elusive foe, difficult to track and even harder to catch when they had a few hours lead on their pursuers.

While this low-intensity war was being prosecuted in South West Africa, an altogether more robust conflict was taking place just north in Angola. South Africa had become embroiled in a hot war with the communist *Movimento Popular de Libertação de Angola* (MPLA) in Angola. At the urging of the United States, a sometime friend of the South Africans, the SADF had in 1975 invaded Angola to prevent a communist takeover of the country when the Portuguese had abandoned their colony to its own devices, literally overnight. The SADF also trained, armed and fed the anti-MPLA factions in Angola. The two independent, and at times antagonistic, factions lined up against the MPLA were the *Frente Nacional para a Libertação de Angola* (FNLA) led by Holden Roberto whose power resided in the fact that he was related to President Mobuto of Zaire; the other was *União Nacional para a Independência Total de Angola* (UNITA) led by the large and blustering Jonas Savimbi.

When the USA reversed its position on supporting the anti-communist forces of the FNLA and UNITA, the South African government decided that fighting the communists in another country was to prove counter-productive since the Americans had lost their nerve. In March 1976, South Africa withdrew from Angola, despite having had its vanguard, again led by Jan Breytenbach, within sight of the Angolan capital, Luanda.

Thus the communist takeover of Angola took place without much ado, with the result that SWAPO now had a sympathetic country on its doorstep from which to operate. It was now able to base its guerrillas in small camps dotted across southern Angola, secure in the belief that international pressure would prevent South Africa from launching trans-border attacks.

SWAPO's military headquarters were still based in Zambia but the Zambian training camps had now become prisons for SWAPO dissidents, of which there were many. One SWAPO group which had earned the displeasure of their leader Sam Nujoma was the Shipanga faction. Andreas Shipanga was an outspoken critic of Nujoma's corrupt practices and his curious decision to support UNITA against the MPLA in the struggle for dominance in Angola. Nujoma had Shipanga imprisoned along with a thousand of his followers when Shipanga urged Nujoma to take the fight to South Africa instead of dilly-dallying in Angola. Shipanga was eventually transferred to a Tanzanian jail because of international pressure on Nujoma to release him. However, Julius Nyerere, the president of Tanzania, was unmoved by international cries for justice for Shipanga. Shipanga's followers, out of the international spotlight, were not as fortunate. They were systematically starved and on one occasion shot at *en masse* by their Zambian guards under orders from Nujoma. Luckily for the prisoners, the Zambians didn't have the stomach for mass murder at someone else's behest, consequently the death toll was low. The survivors will be met later at their last stand at Cassinga.

The UN meanwhile was applying more and more pressure on South Africa to withdraw from South West Africa. Despite SWAPO being an Owambo-only party, the UN had recognized its leader Sam Nujoma as the sole legitimate leader of the country, thereby ignoring all other population groups, indigenous or otherwise. SWAPO therefore found itself with the wholehearted support of the UN.

Overtly the UN championed Nujoma as the authentic leader of South West Africa, while covertly it provided material aid to SWAPO and its armed wing, the People's Liberation Army of Namibia (PLAN), through thinly disguised military training camps masquerading as refugee camps so as to be eligible for UNICEF food, medicines and money. In later chapters we will

Above: Lűderitz, German South West Africa. *Source: Wikicommons*

Right: After the occupation of South West Africa by the Germans a systematic genocide of the Herero people was instituted. *Source: Wikicommons*

see how Soviet and Cuban advisers managed to convince the UN to pay for their surrogate forces by clever manipulation of the humanitarian sentiments of the West.

By early 1978, South Africa had been forced, by the use of a lot of stick and very little carrot, to accede to holding elections for a South West Africa prior to independence. Resolution 435 was adopted by the UN Security Council which meant that a handover of power was a *fait accompli* even though a large portion of the population had been terrorized by SWAPO and had had its leaders murdered.

PLAN had established large bases in Angola in a chain of supply routes and a network of Soviet, Cuban and United Nations support logistics. The primary military camp was Cassinga. This was SWAPO's and PLAN's headquarters in Angola. Cassinga was a classic military base, run along conventional military lines with a hierarchy of military personnel from Regional Commander, Dimo Amaambo, down to the traditional political commissars and cadres (*see* the soldier's notebook, captured at Cassinga, in the chapter 10).

By 1978, there were many other smaller camps scattered about 20 kilometres from the Angolan–South West African border on the Angolan side. A variety of FAPLA and Cuban bases were interspersed among these SWAPO bases, serving to disguise them and lend protection in the event of attack. There was even a smattering of MK in southern Angola as the South African ANC had also started basing some of its cadres in Angola, away from the tentacles of the SADF.

Because of the looming election in South West Africa, SWAPO was keen to have as large a force as possible poised to invade the territory should the election they were reluctantly being pressured into participating in, not go their way. South Africa on the other hand wanted a militarily weak SWAPO to enable them to repulse an armed invasion. At the time, South African forces were hamstrung by UN peacekeeping forces whose support for SWAPO was plainly overt.

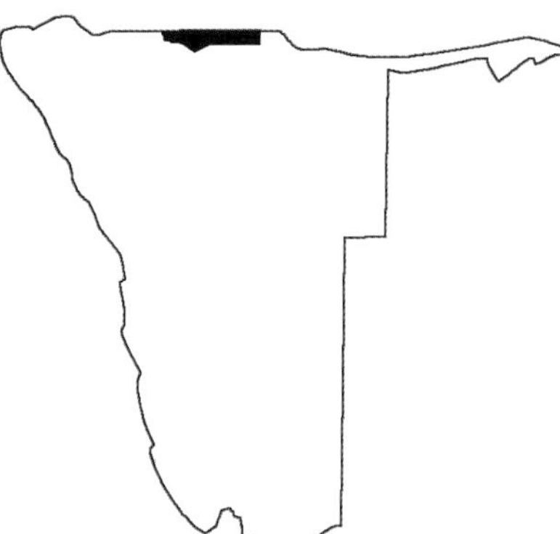

Map of Namibia showing Ovamboland in the far north.
Source: Wikicommons

This was the delicate situation in which the South African cabinet found itself. If it did nothing, everything would be lost, even if the moderate multicultural parties won a majority in the election. A communist neighbour would be the result. If, on the other hand, the South Africans took the bull by the horns and attacked SWAPO, they would be damned by the world as being the aggressor and, moreover, attacking a sovereign state. It is no surprise that the leader of the cabinet, John Vorster, vacillated between supporting his military on the one side and placating his less adventurous ministers on the other.

CHAPTER TWO: PLANNING AND OPERATION *BRUILHOF*

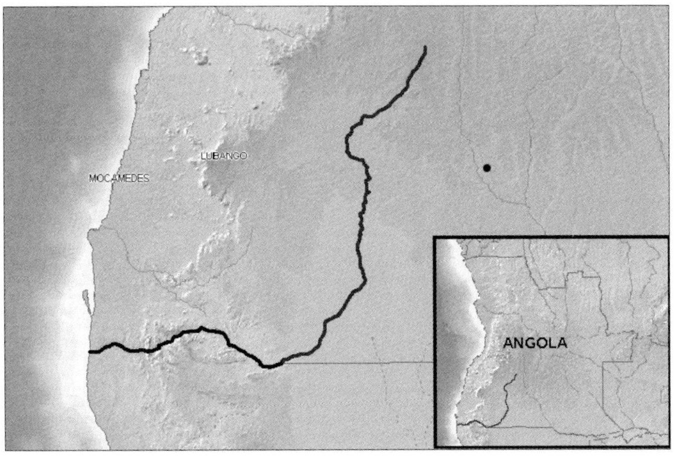

Cunene River, Angola. Cassinga is indicated due east of the river. *Source: Wikicommons*

At the beginning of 1978 the South African Defence Force noticed that there was a big build-up of SWAPO troops and weaponry in the south of Angola, just a few kilometres from the South West African border. It became clear that SWAPO was planning a new offensive with heavy weapons to coincide with the rainy season. While the South Africans felt fairly confident in dealing with this string of small bases spread haphazardly along the border, they were concerned that the source of all this manpower and weaponry was unknown to them.

A flurry of air and ground reconnaissance sorties took place. Canberra photo-reconnaissance aircraft were used to overfly southern Angola at 20,000 feet and systematically photograph every square kilometre. 32 Battalion Reconnaissance Wing foot patrols were sent to scour the bush for evidence of a large base or bases. The Reconnaissance Regiment was also tasked with finding the big prize. What these patrols were looking for was the usual evidence of SWAPO bases hidden in dense bush: footpaths converging on large, well-bushed areas and dirt roads that apparently went nowhere. Increased human activity near known water points and the presence of smoke coming from concealed habitation were some of the signs that would signify an enemy camp. The typical SWAPO camp would be well dug in, camouflaged and difficult to detect. This is how the camps at Chetequera, code-named Vietnam by SWAPO and 30 kilometres north of beacon 9 on the cutline, were found. Vietnam was estimated to house two to three hundred soldiers with a few hundred more in smaller satellite bases dotted around the main base. It was well protected by a maze of trenches and bunkers mainly on the southern side from where an attack would be expected to come. The northeast, or Vietnam's left rear, was fairly open and unprotected by any satellite camps and was plainly vulnerable to a looping conventional attack.

What the South Africans were *not* looking for was an enemy base situated in an established town with military activity disguised as the normal workings of busy townsfolk. SWAPO and their Soviet advisers had pulled a masterstroke of deception out the hat. The town of Cassinga was the Portuguese *Chef de Post* during colonial times and the local hub of a small iron-mining area, but had fallen into disuse during the long Angolan conflict. It was well served by major roads and situated right next to the Culonga River, a tributary of the Cunene, 250 kilometres north of the South West African–Angolan border.

The actual significance of Cassinga was only discovered when a routine Canberra photo-reconnaissance flight brought back a reel of film with one very interesting photograph hidden among the thousands of innocuous ones. One of the interpreters at the Joint Air Reconnaissance Interpretation Centre (JARIC), noticed a familiar outline on a bare piece of land. When the image was enlarged, it proved to be the outline of South West Africa depicted by what looked like whitewashed stones on a parade ground with a flag fluttering in the middle of the outline and hundreds of troops standing on parade around the flag. A SWAPO political commissar had evidently become a little too enthusiastic in his dramatic show-and-tell lesson to the cadres and had unwittingly given the game away.

The South African Truth and Reconciliation Commission Volume 2, Chapter 2, 'The State Outside South Africa between 1960 and 1990' states: "On 8 March 1978, the chief of the army, Lieutenant-General Viljoen, sent a communiqué (H/LEER/309) to the chief of the defence force, in which he identified the camp at Kassinga as the planning headquarters of SWAPO's armed wing, the People's Liberation Army of Namibia (PLAN)—subordinate only to SWAPO's defence headquarters at Lubango. He also noted that the camp was the principal medical centre for the treatment of seriously injured guerrillas, as well as the concentration point for guerrilla recruits being dispatched to training centres in Lubango and Luanda and to operational bases in East and West Cunene. The camp also offered refresher courses in infantry warfare and mine-laying."

The thing that convinced the interpreters was the extensive zigzag trench system that could clearly be seen surrounding the town on three sides. The western side of the town was bordered by a meandering river which was deep and wide in the rainy season, becoming less of a barrier in the drier months. The northern and eastern sides of the base were well protected but the trench system was incomplete on the southern side, presumed still to be under construction.

Now that the big prize had been found, the planning to destroy it immediately began. A headcount of the troops on the parade

After an intensive retraining programme, Colonel Breytenbach (smiling at camera) relaxes with his men at Letaba Ranch.

ground, and estimates made from the number of buildings, both permanent and jerry-rigged, as well as a tent count, yielded an estimate of about 2,000 enemy soldiers living at Cassinga, SWAPO code-name Moscow, together with a few hundred camp followers, comprising prostitutes, wives, girlfriends and a few children. Subsequent follow-up reconnaissance flights brought this estimate to between 1,500 and 3,000 soldiers with up to 300 camp followers.

The reason for the wide difference between the minimum and maximum numbers of soldiers and the static amount of camp followers was that the soldiers' numbers were in a constant state of flux because they were flowing in from Zambia, the USSR and Cuba, where they were being trained and flowing out again, armed and burdened with food and weapons, to head south where they were assembling for the big push into South West Africa. As it transpired, just before the attack on Moscow Base, there was a large influx of about a thousand soldiers into Cassinga who were housed in a hastily erected tent camp. These are now known to be the remnants of the ill-fated Shipanga faction who had been persecuted in a Zambian detention camp before being sent to Cassinga. Intelligence of the planned attack had been received by SWAPO from the super-spy Dieter Gerhardt who was based at the South African Defence Communications Centre at Silvermine in the Cape. Sam Nujoma, leader of SWAPO, had cleverly put his most belligerent but irritating soldiers into a position where they would do maximum damage to the South Africans and if ultimately unsuccessful, would be eliminated as potential opposition to his autocratic rule. It is not surprising therefore that Nujoma has since been reluctant to admit they were there, let alone acknowledge their bravery.

The task of destroying bases Moscow and Vietnam became an imperative as detailed planning began. Chetequera/Vietnam was a relatively simple task. Situated no more than 30 kilometres from the border, it was very vulnerable to a lightning-fast attack by armour and mechanized infantry. If this could be dovetailed with the Moscow attack, the radio-jamming and security precautions could be pooled and become effective for both attacks. Colonel (listed as a Major in *TRC*, p. 1) Frank Bestbier, an old paratrooper and the author's company commander at 1 Parachute Battalion in 1970, would command that attack. General Constand Viljoen, Chief of the Army, decided that he needed South Africa's most experienced combat soldier to lead the attack on Cassinga as the risks involved were great, with the base 250 kilometres from the safety of South West Africa. The troops to be used were to be almost exclusively Civilian Force (territorial) paratroopers. If anything went wrong, as is historically prone in an airborne assault, the political price to pay would be enormous. The general summoned Jan Breytenbach and informed him of his new command. Operation *Bruilof* was born and Colonel Breytenbach quickly began his estimation of what was needed in order to capture and destroy Cassinga, SWAPO's flagship base Moscow, but more importantly, what would be needed to extract his paratroopers after the battle.

Initially, Colonel Breytenbach estimated that a force of 450 paratroopers would be needed to accomplish the task. This presumed that surprise would be complete and pressing home the assault would be immediate on the paratroopers landing. It also presupposed that the air force would pound the base effectively with anti-personnel and high-explosive bombs.

The Infantry Handbook stipulates that an attacking force of two and a half times the defending force be used on a fortified position but Colonel Breytenbach was confident his paratroopers could do without numerical superiority and still prevail.

During the exhaustive planning and war-gaming process, it was found that although there would be no difficulty providing 450 paratroopers and delivering them to fortress Cassinga, extracting them would prove impossible. While seven C-130s or C-160s would be needed to transport the 450 paratroopers there, it would take 38 helicopters to transport them back and there were only 18 helicopters available. This meant that only 210 troops could be lifted to safety, leaving 240 paratroopers to face a possible 4,000 enemy troops; it was too much to ask.

The idea of extracting the troops in two waves was then conceived. This meant that the maximum number capable of being lifted out was still 30 short of Colonel Breytenbach's minimum of 450 needed to do the job. This problem was further exacerbated by General Viljoen insisting on bringing back the used parachutes. Just the parachutes and their recovery bags would fill a large number of helicopters. To make the dual-wave extraction work, a Helicopter Administration Area (HAA) would need to be established not more than 30 kilometres from Cassinga, which would need to be stocked with fuel and manned by a guard squad, further complicating the planning.

Because of the reduced helicopter capacity, the number of paratroopers which could be extracted was reduced to 343. This was close to becoming an unacceptable number to Colonel Breytenbach so he took the only route he could to even the odds, which was to convince the air force to beef up their initial bombing attack so as to hopefully reduce the number of enemy as well as to further disorient them and make their defence less effective. The air force needed little convincing, so planning proceeded with a sharply reduced assault force taken into account.

When Colonel Breytenbach accepted the challenge from General Viljoen, he was told to proceed immediately to Letaba Ranch, a piece of land familiar to the colonel. It had been within his area of responsibility when working in the Pretoria area. Letaba Ranch was a huge piece of land which bordered the Kruger National Park on its western boundary near the town of Phalaborwa. It was an ideal spot to conceal a few hundred paratroopers and retrain them to the levels of fitness and combat readiness required for a daring raid. At this time the raid was codenamed *Bruilof*, or 'wedding' in Afrikaans. The primary objective at this stage was to undertake an airborne assault on the Chetequera complex of enemy camps about 30 kilometres north of the South West African border, with Cassinga being the secondary. There were two main camps, one of which was Chetequera, with the other objective being 20 kilometres to the east. Two parallel lines of paratroopers were to drop on either side of these camps, one a stopper group, the other an assault group. The assault group was to advance and force the defenders onto the stopper groups and thus eliminate the enemy.

The paratroopers, who had already been called up, were the entire Citizen Force complement of paratroopers, comprising 2 and 3 Parachute Battalions. Many of these troops were older, seasoned soldiers who had completed many three-month stints on Fire Force duties, flying out of Ondangwa in Owamboland to hotspots all over South West Africa to follow up and chase down SWAPO who had infiltrated from Zambia or Angola and committed terrorist atrocities against the local population. Many of the men were quite a bit older than 30, a ripe old age for the hardships of a combat paratrooper.

The climate at Letaba Ranch was stiflingly hot with very little breeze. Accommodation was in tents with ramshackle stretchers. The food was ordinary as a small field kitchen tried valiantly to cater for the hundreds of hungry paratroopers. Training concentrated on fire and movement and house clearing as this was what was envisaged as the primary task of the assault companies. The stopper groups were going to be doing a lot of fire and no movement, but this didn't prevent the instructors from making the troops go through the endless exercises, all with live ammunition to promote realism and emphasize the importance of fire control. A few hours a day were dedicated to long runs and calisthenics in the oppressive, damp heat of the Transvaal Lowveld (now Kruger-Lowveld). Digging latrines was also considered excellent exercise for battle-ready troops in waiting. A few training jumps were scheduled which entailed a bumpy truck ride from Letaba Ranch to the Pietersburg air base where the paratroopers emplaned and jumped into the adjacent air force firing range to practise form-up drills and fire and movement. Colonel Breytenbach's edict of 'train hard—fight easy' was being stretched to inhuman lengths in the heat of the late Lowveld summer. The jumps went without too much incident, with a few broken arms and legs and a few parachutes irretrievably entangled in the low, flat-topped thorn trees which studded the area. In one instance, a Bedford truck was recruited to try and pull a parachute out of a tree, only to see the whole tree yanked out of the ground before it would stubbornly yield the parachute.

Toward the end of the retraining period, with D-Day approaching, the colonel threw an impromptu party for the troops and officers in the bush alongside the Letaba River which gave the ranch its name. In the heat of the day, much beer was consumed and the less fleet-footed officers, including the colonel, were thrown into the hippo- and crocodile-infested river from the high banks. Luckily this loud assault on their domain shocked the fauna into inaction as the victims emerged howling with laughter and set about hurling their erstwhile attackers into the river in return.

The high spirits of the paratroopers were severely dampened the next day when they were informed by a somewhat hung-over officer corps that Operation *Bruilof* had been postponed due to a security leak which they intimated might have come from one of the troops sneaking off to make a telephone call home while in Pietersburg. This was only found to be untrue many years later when the spy Dieter Gerhardt was debriefed and found to have intercepted a message about *Bruilof* and passed it on to his Soviet masters who in turn advised SWAPO that an airborne assault was imminent on some of their camps. A reconnaissance flight over the target had picked up preparations for an attack and the operation was called off as a result. This was not the first time the paratroopers had been disappointed by a cancelled mission and it would not be the last. As this was to have been a proper airborne assault, it was doubly disappointing. The next day, the paratroopers were flown back to Pretoria whence they would make their own way home.

Just a few weeks later, some of paratroopers were called up again. This time they were told that it was for Operation *Quicksilver*, a massive combined military exercise to take place at Smitsdrift near Kimberley. The paratroopers didn't know it at the time but *Quicksilver* was a deception, not only to make the enemy believe that a call-up of paratroopers was only for a training exercise, but to keep all the foreign diplomatic invitees observing *Quicksilver* out of the way while the real operation was taking place. This new and more ambitious plan was named Operation *Reindeer*. The *Bruilof* plan had by now been expanded to incorporate the attack on Cassinga as the main objective. It had become patently clear that Cassinga was in fact the prize.

CHAPTER THREE: TRAINING AT DE BRUG

The planned day of the assault was 1 May. The reason for this was that May Day is traditionally an important communist holiday, Workers' Day. It was a day when the real Moscow in Russia held their vast military parades and it was hoped that SWAPO would uphold the tradition and hold a big parade at Cassinga in honour of the day. When the film from a small camera captured at Cassinga was later developed, it was in fact shown that a big parade had indeed been held, with posters of Lenin and Marx being prominently displayed.

With D-Day looming, it was time for Colonel Breytenbach to thin out the numbers of paratroopers in the training area. As usual, more paratroopers had turned up for the 'exercise' than the amount called up. If there were ever rumours of action surrounding a call-up of the predominantly Civilian Force paratroopers, word spread like a virus and every paratrooper who could convince family and employer to again suffer his absence, would turn up at the rally point. This time the endless repetitiveness of the training and the seeming pointlessness of it all worked in the colonel's favour. Many troops were disillusioned after the cancellation of *Bruilof* and quite ready to call it a day and return to civvy life. The full strength was assembled on the makeshift parade ground in the veld at De Brug as the colonel offered anyone who wanted to leave an immediate lift to the station to return home that day. Sufficient paratroopers had had enough to make the requisite reduction and, to their eternal regret, were cheerfully sent on their way.

The camp was immediately sealed off: no further traffic was allowed in or out, MPs were diplomatically posted on the entry and exit routes in order to keep the area effectively quarantined until D-Day. Colonel Breytenbach then called together the remaining troops, who by now had been supplemented by a platoon of national servicemen (NSM) from 1 Parachute Battalion who were to supply a mortar group which the combined 2 and 3 Parachute Battalions did not have because of the selective call-up. The colonel switched off the public-address system in order to keep his words from being broadcast and, in his inimitably dry style, informed the reduced force that they had, by electing to stay at De Brug, selected themselves for a combat jump into Angola. After a moment of absolute silence while the news was digested, the paratroopers burst into raucous cheering which was only silenced by a low-level fly-past of a formation of C-130 and C-160 aircraft, the same aircraft that were to carry them into battle. It was a dramatic end to the colonel's speech, providing a taste of the sound and fury that in a few days was to follow.

Broad smiles and excited chatter showed that the dream of every paratrooper was to come true for these lucky few. A combat jump deep behind enemy lines; it was what they had trained for but had all but given up hoping to achieve. Much of the paratrooping role was taken up in deploying by helicopter in the modern, or reaction force, context with the opportunities for the traditional paratrooper attack very few and far between. The jubilation among the paratroopers was also due to the long string of disappointments and cancellations of operations, the most recent of which was Operation *Bruilof* of just five weeks before, which was now the precursor to what would become famous as Operation *Reindeer*.

Long before the colonel's announcement, in the shed near the old farmhouse, a scale model of the target had been completed. Every trench, barrack building, bunker and administration block was reproduced in three dimensions. Trees and bushes, grass, river and the parade ground were all there. The scale model would have been worthy of display at Harrods Toyland, had there been an electric train set included. This entire model-making process had taken place under strict security, but even the duller-witted paratroopers had soon begun to suspect that something out of the ordinary was afoot: the camp was too secure and too tense for the routine Operation *Quicksilver*.

A briefing was called in the shed. The whole command structure crammed into the dim little space, in the centre of which was a large 3m x 5m model. Each company commander together with his platoon commander was seated in the area corresponding to approximately where he and his men would land.

Captain Johan Blaauw, commander of the platoon of 1 Parachute Battalion national servicemen sat at the northern end where his task was to subdue the north of Cassinga before linking up with Captain Piet Botes to form the northern line of stoppers. Captains Gerrie Steyn and Hugo Murray sat together on the western side where their companies, A and B respectively, would form the assault group which was to sweep through the camp, driving the enemy onto the stopper groups surrounding the camp. Commandant Monty Brett sat on the eastern side where his stopper groups would cut off any avenue of escape for those SWAPO guerrillas who did not stand and fight. Captain Tommie Lamprecht sat at the southern end of the shed together with Lieutenant Pierre Hough, the Anti-Tank Platoon leader, who with his mines and RPGs would guard the southern entrance to the camp against possible interference by Cuban armour, based 20 kilometres away at Techamutete.

Commandant Lew Gerber, Doctor Rassie Erasmus, the forward air controllers (Commandant Blikkies Blignaut and Major Frans Botes), Lieutenant Piet Nel of the Mortar Platoon, the Signals Officer (WOII Blommetjie Blom) and RSM Erasmus formed the HQ component under Colonel Breytenbach.

All stared at the brightly lit model in the dusty shed. With the zigzag trenches and bunker systems, the town of Cassinga looked like a First World War fortress, protected on three sides by the

Paratroopers try to snatch a couple of hours' sleep amid kit and parachutes.

04h00: paras fitting their parachutes and equipment, Grootfontein hangar.

had been deserted because of the ongoing conflict. The big prize had, at last, been found and it had been under the noses of the SADF for some time. The outline of South West Africa, noted initially by the photo analyzer, was only a temporary layout on the parade ground made from stones, presumably as a political display or instructional aid. It never appeared again and it was sheer luck that it was picked up by the high-altitude surveillance of the South African Air Force. Planning for an attack had started immediately when confirmation was obtained as to the military importance of the base.

The town of Cassinga is more than 250 kilometres from the South West African border with Angola. Between Cassinga and the border were many smaller bases and villages which would act as early-warning alarms were Cassinga attacked conventionally by an armoured column or mobile infantry. The obvious means of attack would be by air strike; this would certainly cause much damage but would gather no intelligence and documentation that a major SWAPO base would be expected to yield. The planners had begun thinking along the lines of a joint air strike and paratroop assault on the

trench system and on the fourth by a wide, fast-flowing river.

As mentioned, the reason why SWAPO's main training and logistics camp had been undetected for so long was that the SADF had expected SWAPO camps to follow the usual pattern of being hidden in thick bush and well spread out over a large area. These types of camp could only be detected by foot patrols or by very careful study of aerial photographs that could sometimes reveal patterns of footpaths or livestock trails leading to and from heavily bushed areas. Cassinga was the complete antithesis of the usual SWAPO camp, in that it was once a Portuguese mining town that

base. This was all fairly straightforward in the assault phase of an operation but the withdrawal phase was still proving problematic. As mentioned, the military handbooks stipulate that in an attack on a fortified base, the attacking force should outnumber the defenders by at least two and a half to one. Cassinga base had as many as 4,000 defenders at any one time and an attacking force of 10,000 paratroopers was neither possible nor practical.

The South African Truth and Reconciliation Commission Volume 2, Chapter 2, 'The State Outside South Africa between 1960 and 1990' quotes:

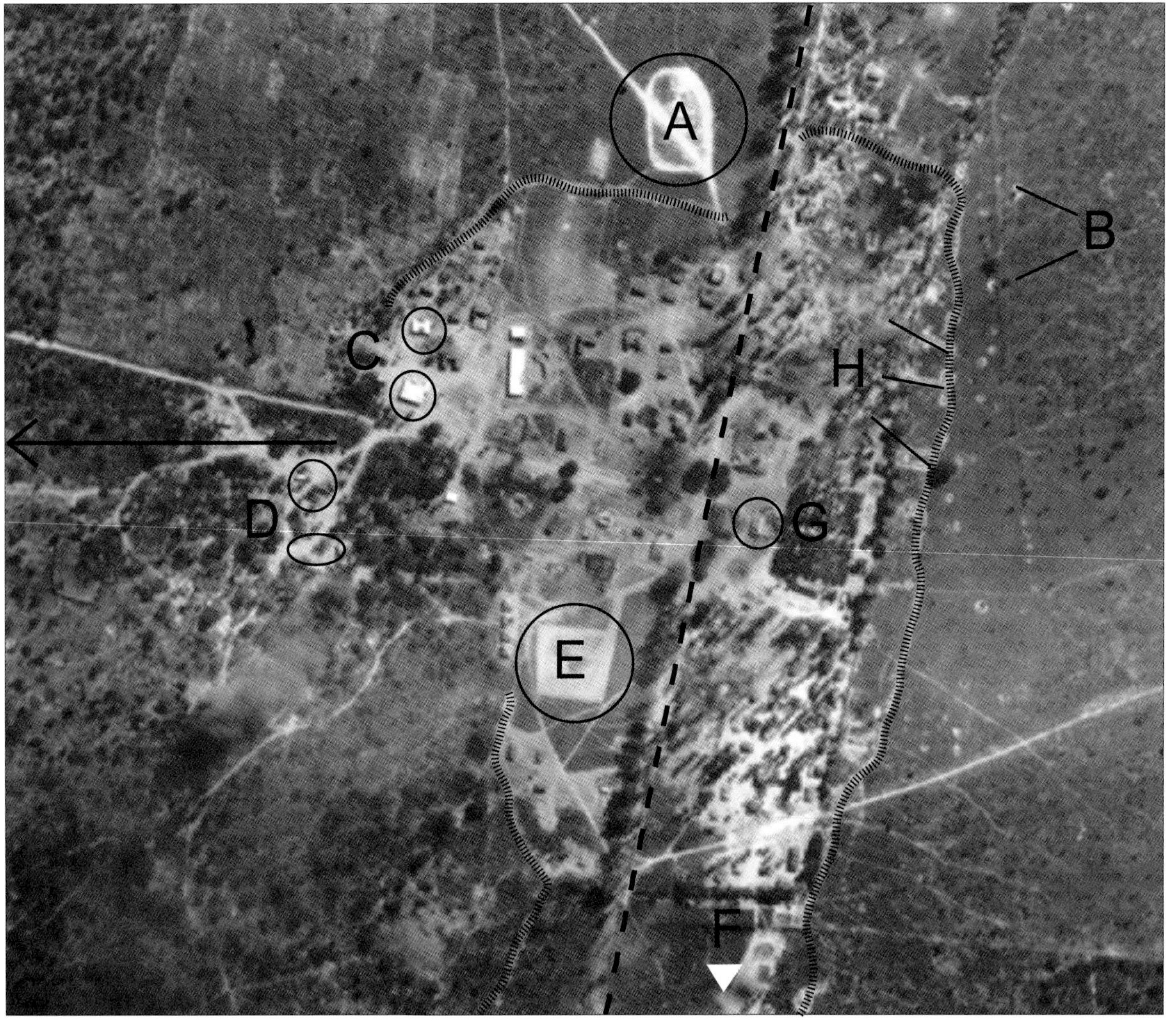

Cassinga Base aerial photograph

---- North–south road between Cuvango and Techamutete
⟵ Culonga River runs 960m due west from the centre of Cassinga town
IIIIIIIII Defensive trenches
A: Sports fields
B: Forward foxholes
C: New vehicle park and workshops, both are flat-roofed, permanent buildings
D: Old vehicle park with a concentration of vehicles, including a bus and an office building
E: Parade square
F: South toward the Engineer Complex
G: Largest permanent building, identified as the PLAN headquarters
H: Communication/access trenches

There were three designated target areas for this operation. The bombing runs would come in from the north and firstly take out targets C and D, secondly targets A and E, before finally attacking targets B, H, G and F.

Approval for the Kassinga operation—which became part of Operation *Reindeer*—was received in about March 1978. The original operational orders included the following priorities and instructions:

A. Maximum losses were to be inflicted on the enemy but, where possible, leaders must be captured and brought out. Once the attack was completed, no prisoner of war was to be shot in cold blood.
B. Documents as well as useful weapons were to be removed.
C. Bases were to be destroyed.
D. Skirmishes with Cuban and Angolan army forces were to be avoided if at all possible.
E. Photographs were to be taken after the attack to counter enemy allegations.
F. Where possible, women and children were not to be shot.

As planning progressed, it was felt that the element of surprise, coupled with an effective air strike, could be such a potent force-multiplier that a very much smaller attacking force could be successful. The German airborne attack on the Belgian fort, Eben-Emael, during the Second World War had shown this could be done. But the paratroopers could not be expected to walk 250 kilometres back to safety after disturbing a hornet's nest across the whole of southern Angola, having expended most of their ammunition and carrying the inevitable casualties. This meant that the number of paratroopers who could be sent in to the attack was in fact the amount that could feasibly be extracted by helicopter after the battle. Even if there were sufficient helicopters to carry enough troops out, there were other, seemingly insurmountable problems that a heliborne withdrawal presented. A 500-kilometre round trip, half of which would be under fully loaded, hot and high-altitude conditions, was not a physical possibility. The helicopters did not have that kind of capability and there would certainly not be enough fuel for the circling and holding patterns the small landing zones identified at Cassinga would demand.

Innovative thinking was required and it was forthcoming in the concept of a Helicopter Administration Area (HAA). The idea was that a temporary base would be established near Cassinga but well out of earshot where a refuelling depot could operate. This would provide a number of advantages to the attacking force. The HAA would enable the helicopters to refuel either en route to Cassinga or on the way home, it would also provide flexibility in an area where half the force could be withdrawn to safety and the helicopters could return and collect the other half. This would double the number of paratroopers who could be extracted from the battlefield and thus double the number who could be inserted.

The plan thus evolved into a two-stage withdrawal where after the battle half the force and any casualties would be withdrawn to the South African air force base at Ondangwa in South West Africa. After refuelling at the HAA, the helicopters would then return for the other half. Naturally, this plan would only work if the paratroopers were victorious because, if they were not, there would be no safe landing zone for the helicopters from which to extract troops. For the paratroopers the plan was simple: win or walk. The walk home would mean a fighting retreat of over 250 kilometres with very little food and water and even less ammunition.

The HAA selected was 19 kilometres from Cassinga and out of a flight path which would alert the Cuban detachment with their MiG fighter jets and armour at Techamutete to the south. The Cuban garrison was constantly borne in mind during the planning phase and it was hoped to keep them completely out of the picture by jamming radio communications in southern Angola during the duration of the battle. This was accomplished fairly successfully on the day by using an EW Skymaster DC-4 aircraft crammed with electronic listening and jamming devices patrolling the border area.

The South African Truth and Reconciliation Commission Volume 2, Chapter 2, 'The State Outside South Africa between 1960 and 1990' quotes: "Finally, [it was] suggested that, given the presence in the camp of PLAN's commander, Dimo Amaambo, important documents could be captured. Other documents in the SADF files make it clear that it was also hoped that Amaambo and other senior PLAN officials would be captured or killed."

The discovery of Cassinga as SWAPO's headquarters in southern Angola also raised the hope that the paratroopers would find Sapper Johan van der Mescht, an engineer who had been captured some months earlier in South West Africa when a SWAPO raiding party slipped past the infantry detachment guarding the engineers, killing two and capturing van der Mescht, taking him back to Angola. It later transpired that van der Mescht had been imprisoned at Cassinga but was transferred to Luanda before the attack took place. (A Swedish photographer took some photos of him at Cassinga during a photo shoot which is today viewable on the SWAPO archive website, together with photographs of mothers with babies and rifles on their backs.)

A last training jump was scheduled to take place at De Brug two days before D-Day. Colonel Breytenbach was in Pretoria at the time sorting out the last-minute details with the air force. Brigadier du Plessis stood in for the colonel on the day but the jump turned into a shambles with misplaced companies and stopper groups. All in all, very good practice for what was about to happen at Cassinga.

Two days later, the paratroopers were flown from Bloemspruit AFB near Bloemfontein to Grootfontein AFB in South West Africa. They landed in the early evening, hungry and thirsty. They were greeted with their overnight accommodation, a hangar on the airfield, and a welcome hot meal of steak and chips with a beer for every man. The meal was produced by the 'Dankie Tannies', the 'Thank You Aunts', of Grootfontein. (Like the WVS, the Women's Voluntary Service, Dankie Tannies were volunteers, mothers of troops on the border who assembled food parcels and writing materials for distribution to the men in the bush. They also welcomed troop trains at stations on the way to Windhoek from South Africa with refreshments and snacks.) The hangar had been pre-prepared for the paratroopers with their parachutes neatly laid out in their chalks, or sticks, in the order in which they would jump. A detachment of Permanent Force (Regular Army) dispatchers had preceded them to Grootfontein and meticulously set up their gear, each main parachute leaning on its corresponding reserve parachute, all annotated and numbered with each paratrooper's name, position in stick, rank, reserve number and main parachute number.

(This entire Fit 'Chute List is published in Colonel Breytenbach's book, *Eagle Strike*.)

CHAPTER FOUR: SKILLIE HUMAN'S DISTURBING PREMONITION AND THE JUMP

Like a guillotine blade, running up its rails, the side doors of the Hercules slowly ascend. The widening aperture blasts eye-watering oblongs of daylight into the dim interior of the aircraft. A rush of fresh air swooshes and eddies down the fuselage, bringing welcome cool to the paratroopers sweating under their steel helmets and heavy combat loads.

May 4 1978

05h19: Four Canberra bombers take off from Waterkloof AFB in Pretoria; they fly over Rundu in the far eastern part of South West Africa before turning northwest toward Cassinga.

05h43: Four Buccaneers take off, also from Waterkloof. One of them, armed with 72 68mm SNEB rockets, lands at Grootfontein to refuel and remain on standby for close support if required.

Earlier, at Grootfontein, the troops had marched out of the hangar in the darkened chill of an early winter morning. Long parallel lines of numbered sticks in reverse jump order: first in, last out. The nine huge transport aircraft loomed out of the murk, tail-on to the paratroopers, their interiors making cosy islands of dim yellow light on the bleak, grey concrete apron. The small step up onto the ramp felt impossibly difficult for the troops weighed down with a T10 main parachute, reserve parachute clipped to tightly adjusted harnesses and all the paraphernalia of battle hanging about the webbing and pockets of the jumpers. Twenty magazines of full-house 7.62 ammunition, a couple of 100-round belts of LMG ammo for the section light machine guns, a double handful of M26 grenades distributed around the kidney pouches and a brace of phosphorus grenades, useful in bunker-clearing and signalling with their billowing clouds of bright, white smoke. Some carried medic kits loaded with the dead weight of saline drips while others bore clusters of 60mm mortar bombs. Some had RPGs and all had several water bottles and their personal weapons strapped to their sides. The Anti-Tank Platoon was further burdened by the cumbersome number 8 'cheese' mines which would be laid to protect the paratroopers from the Cuban armour stationed at Techamutete. A few days' worth of emergency rations, and in Rifleman McWilliams's case, a six-pack of beer cans wrapped in a wet sandbag (a 'bush fridge') and ten packets of cigarettes distributed to every pocket completed the burden. These luxuries were meant for self-consumption as well as trade if it eventuated that the attacking force had to walk home. Cigarettes and beer would be worth their weight in diamonds on a long fighting withdrawal. There were no scales at Grootfontein, so no one knew how much weight they carried, but the effort needed to climb that small step onto the aircraft ramp told of the discomfort in the plane and hard landings to come.

The interior of the aircraft had the familiar comforting aroma of musty webbing, a hint of disinfectant and the faintest trace of dried vomit. A last-minute reiteration of the battle plan in the hangar was accompanied by motivational talks from the officers. Some were of a religious nature and some less so.

Skillie Human, a married paratrooper who had left his wife and daughter to attend yet another 'camp' had a disturbing premonition in the hangar at Grootfontein. Although he could not put it into words, he was very agitated about the dream he had had while restlessly slumbering on the hangar floor the night before the jump. Noticing his distress, a fellow paratrooper got hold of Human's company commander and said that perhaps he should have a word with Human. The company commander took Human aside and asked what the problem was. Human told him that he had had a vivid vision of himself dying the next day at Cassinga.

His company commander had a long chat with him and said that many people were anxious about the battle, but that everything would be all right on the day and that Human would forget all about it as soon as he exited the aircraft the next morning. A somewhat mollified Human returned to his platoon and although still clearly upset, continued with his battle preparations. His distress caused a ripple among his comrades but was soon forgotten in the excitement of the moment.

His behaviour was completely out of character in that he was a long-time paratrooper with plenty of Fire Force combat experience. He was from a military family and although a quiet type, was always at the forefront when combat was mentioned. As it turned out, whatever was bothering Human was real enough, because after exiting the aircraft over Cassinga, he was never seen again. There is no clue as to what happened to him. His body was never found, not by the paratroopers or the enemy after the battle. The best guess is that he landed in the river and drowned under the heavy burden of his weapon and ammunition.

While interviewing a former SADF soldier who had visited Cassinga in 2010, the author learned that the group of ex-soldiers doing a battlefield tour had questioned a local inhabitant who lived across the river from the ruins of Cassinga. This man was able to confirm many known facts about the battle and told the tourists that his family had recovered two bodies from the river after the battle. The South African forces only had one MIA—Skillie Human—so the other body could have been a SWAPO soldier who had tried fleeing across the river and drowned. The local unfortunately could not remember where the bodies were buried. Numerologists will find it interesting that both people

A rare sight in African skies, six Buccaneers in close formation.
Source: From Fledgling to Eagle

The Canberra.
Source: From Fledgling to Eagle

A Mirage FIII CZ awaits its pilot.
Source: From Fledgling to Eagle

who jumped number 13 in pilot 'Tinkie' Jones's C-130 were killed in action that day.

Captain Steyn of A Company, one of the attack companies, had the foresight to bring along a dog-eared pocket edition of Shakespeare's *Henry V*, paraphrasing Henry's speech before the Battle of Agincourt in Afrikaans-accented English, which did nothing to detract from the stirring words. In his pre-jump briefing, Captain Steyn read:

He that outlives this day, and comes safe home,
Will stand a tiptoe when this day is nam'd.
And rouse him at the name of Crispian.
He that shall live this day, and see old age,
Will yearly on the vigil feast his neighbours,
And say "To-morrow is Saint Crispian."
Then he will strip his sleeve and show his scars,
And say "These wounds I had on Crispian's Day."

This story shall the good man teach his son;
And Crispin Crispian shall ne'er go by,
From this day to the ending of the world,
But we in it shall be remembered—
We few, we happy few, we band of brothers;
For he to-day that sheds his blood with me
Shall be my brother …

It was not Saint Crispin or Crispian's Day, but it was 40 days after Easter Sunday: Ascension Day, Thursday, 4 May 1978.

06h00: The paratrooper task force leaves Grootfontein for Cassinga. Four Hercules C-130s and five Transall C-160s maintain low altitude in order to avoid enemy radar. Two C-130s carrying the reserve force peel off and maintain a holding pattern south of the Angolan–South West African border.

As is customary among paratroopers, the take-off was accompanied by the usual raucous paratrooper singing and clapping of hands in the cramped interior, the heavy aircraft taking the full length of the runway to ease itself into the air. At last, the paratroopers were on their way. This operation, with its stops and starts, its moments of elation and its depressing postponements was finally happening, and 'the happy few' in the lumbering aircraft were about to experience what every paratrooper dreams of: a mass combat jump into enemy territory. These opportunities are few and often decades apart. Legendary names like Normandy, Arnhem, Crete and Dien Bien Phu are part of airborne lore. Many of these operations are not as successful as their planners would have liked, but nonetheless, for paratroopers, names to get the blood up and the jaw set. The Parabats had trained for years for this moment and it was undeniably and breathlessly upon them.

The momentum of events was now irrevocably set on emptying the plane over a belligerent fortified enemy base. An armed force, which greatly outnumbered the Parabats, was housed in a veritable

There can be nothing more frightening than a Canberra passing overhead at 300 feet. *Source: From Fledgling to Eagle*

08h02: Canberra bombing run over Cassinga signals the commencement of the attack.

fortress of defensive trenches and bunkers, a fortress which the Parabats knew could be taken as long as they did not falter and pressed home their advantages of surprise and ferocity—surprise borne of the fact that SWAPO had never before been attacked and enveloped from the sky and ferocity borne of the knowledge that there was no way out for the paratroopers without winning the battle. The prospect of a 250-kilometre hike through enemy territory, seething with hostility and superior firepower, lent strength to their resolve. It must be said that there was little doubt among the paratroopers that they would overcome. During the years of low-intensity war leading up to this battle, South African paratroopers were accustomed to unfavourable odds. All had, from time to time played the role of Fire Force or Reaction Force where a single section of seven or eight paratroopers would hunt down as many as 30 or 40 guerrillas. These experiences perhaps created a false sense of optimism within the paratroopers.

06h30: A DC-4 ELINT\EW and two Puma helicopters, one of which carries the Chief of the South African Army, Lieutenant-General Constand Viljoen, depart from Omauni in South West Africa. The DC-4 takes up a holding pattern south of the Angolan border, intercepting Angolan, Cuban and SWAPO radio transmissions and jamming their communication networks just before the start of the battle. The Pumas are tasked with setting up the HAA, code-named Whiskey 3 and approximately 19 kilometres east of Cassinga. The Mobile Air Operations Team (MAOT) set up radios and navigational beacons at the HAA and signal the all-clear for the rest of the force, comprising the rest of the Hawk Group protection element (31 paratroopers), six medical personnel, two further members of the MAOT and 86 x 200-litre drums of helicopter fuel, all on board a fleet of five Super Frelon and ten Puma helicopters. The helicopters remain at the HAA, ready to extract the task force after the battle.

The aircraft seating plan of four rows of seats running the length of the load compartment left very little room for the dispatchers to move up and down the fuselage to check gear and ensure that all the jumpers were squared away without flapping straps or trailing utility cords which could cause complications when it was time to jump. These dispatchers, all familiar to the troops as Permanent Force NCOs from 1 Parachute Battalion, their mother unit, had been the troops' feared and respected instructors years before when undertaking national service; today they were bustling mother hens, concerned for the troops' welfare and comfort, a strange reversal of roles and a little unsettling for the Citizen Force types who were on their way to the 'sharp end', leaving these paragons of full-time military virtue behind in the aircraft. A legend was created when, because of the long flight, a paratrooper needed to shed the unbearable build-up of urine in his bladder. There are no toilet facilities in the load compartment and in any case it is impossible for a fully laden paratrooper to negotiate the cramped isles to get anywhere except out the door when his turn comes to jump. Here was seen a tough-as-nails Permanent Force staff sergeant unbuttoning a soldier's trousers and gently holding a can at his crotch so that he could relieve himself. Not only did the sergeant re-button the soldier's fly, but to the loud jeers and off-colour catcalls of the rest of the plane's occupants, shook the excess droplets off before stowing the blushing soldier's wedding tackle back where it belonged.

07h00: A Cessna C185 airborne observation post and radio-relay (Telstar) leaves Ondangwa for Cassinga. As the Canberras and Buccaneers fly well east of the target, the Hercules C-130s

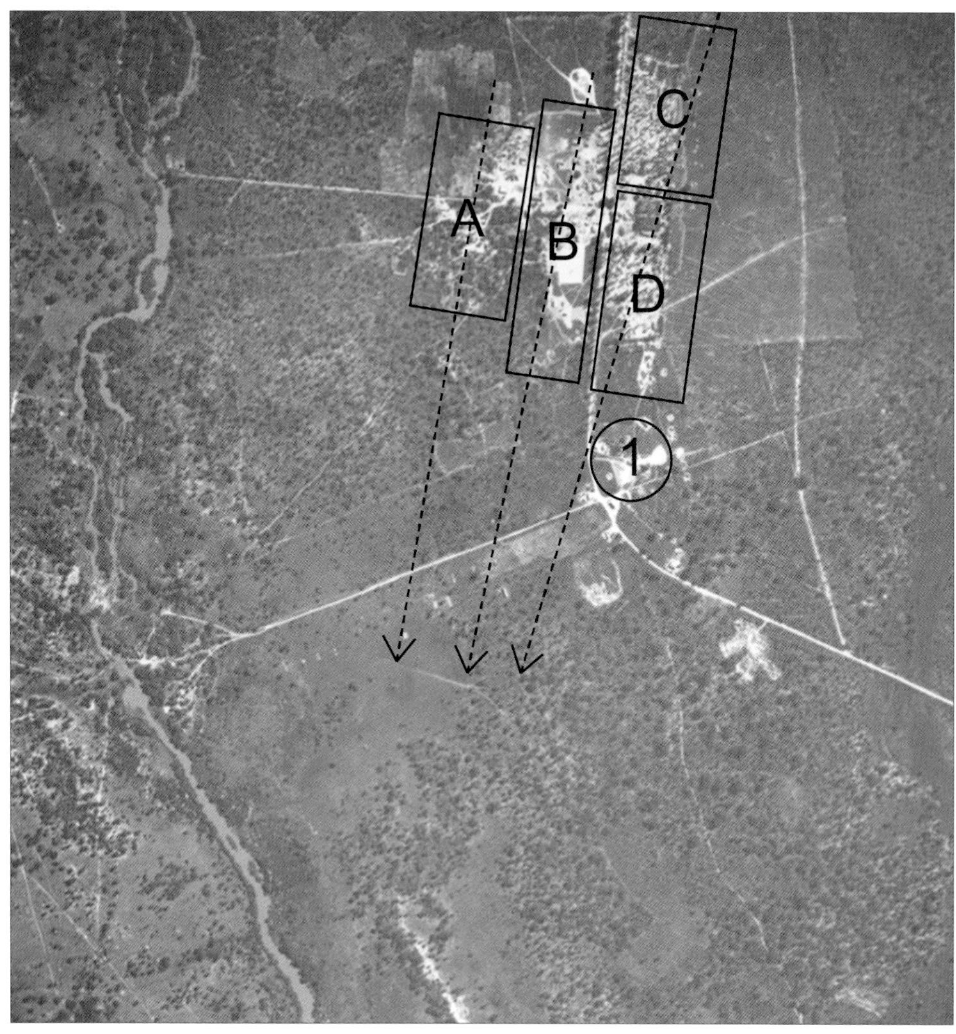

<--- indicates the direction of the bombing runs of the aircraft, north to south.

A/B/C/D: four designated target areas, one for each of the Buccaneers; the fifth, or Recruits' Camp, is not designated.

23 bomb craters were identified, seven of which fell completely wide of the target areas, with the Engineer Complex (1) receiving no hits at all.

Target area A received no hits which is probably due to the fact that that Buccaneer experienced a brake-system malfunction prior to take-off, causing a delay and making it impossible for it to participate in the initial strike. As it turned out, this is where the anti-aircraft guns were entrenched and encountered by the paratroopers. However, within target area A, smoke billowed from the vehicle park, probably a fuel storage dump hit by a strafing Mirage. Vehicles in this area also suffered damage during the strike.

In target area B, various permanent buildings were destroyed by direct hits.

and Transall C-160s carrying the paratroopers go into a holding pattern over the Cubango River, north of Cassinga.

07h50: Two Mirage III CZ fighters take off from Ondangwa AFB and fly toward Cassinga. (The Mirage strike was initially not part of the operation, but was brought into the attack when a recruit camp was identified northwest of the base.)

If a jumper craned his neck to look around and out of one of the miserable little porthole windows of the Hercules, he could see the other five blacked-out aircraft flying in loose formation like a pod of whales in a murky sea, a neighbour sometimes a little higher, sometimes lower, all bound for a far and alien shore. The flight droned on, hour after hour, close and hot, uncomfortable and now silent, with each paratrooper caught up in his own thoughts, memorizing the actions and commands which are the prelude to every jump, then going over the individual tasks and planned movements once on the ground.

Activity from the dispatchers warns of pending action. They test, for the last time, the anchors of the cables to which all the static lines are to be clipped. They tighten the straps on their elephant-grey freefall parachute containers, worn in case of accidental ejection from the aircraft. They fasten monkey-belts attached to the aircraft while they dispatch the jumpers.

All too soon, the command "Stand up, hook up!" is bellowed by the dispatchers, followed by a groaning, grunting, heaving movement all along the aisles while paratroopers try to get into an upright position. Some are helped to their feet by a buddy while some help themselves by climbing up a comrade, and sometimes collapsing him in the process. The static line clips are clipped to the overhead cables and little fiddly safety pins inserted through the microscopic holes in the clips. Eventually, all are standing with the seats folded back to create a little more space and, as usual, the paratroopers find that they have again been sucker-punched by the oldest army trick of all: hurry-up-and-wait.

08h00: In Cassinga, the inhabitants of the base are gathered on the parade ground for the daily roll-call.

Bowed under the weight of equipment, the delay feels like hours. Many paratroopers have sneakily hung some of their burden on a folded seat, some on the protruding baggage of a buddy. All are uncomfortable from the early morning turbulence of the treetop altitude, at times doubling their weight and at others floating them weightless for a few moments before buckling their knees again.

The ten-minute warning is shouted and mimed with ten fingers on out-stretched hands and repeated by everyone. Then the "Check equipment!" order, again chorused by the troops, is yelled out. The mumbled equipment check is then recited by all the jumpers.

Paratroopers jumping from the side doors of a Transall C-160.
Source: From Fledgling to Eagle

These two paratroopers, drifting dangerously toward the river, are also under enemy anti-aircraft fire.

08h07: a Transall C-160 drops its troops over Cassinga.

"Helmet"—check that it is properly fastened—tight—and pulls your jaw back till you look like a chinless wonder from HQ.

"Reserve"—check that it is securely clipped to the harness D-rings and that the handle is not lolling out of its housing, seductively waiting to snag on something and create havoc at the door.

"Quick-release box"—check that the leg-strap clips are inserted and the safety prong is in place in this cynically named lump of hardware.

"Static line free"—check the jumper in front has not snarled his static line on a protruding rifle barrel or wrapped it around his neck, gallows style.

"Pack closure"—ensure that the break cord on the outside of the pack of the jumper in front has not broken, threatening to cause just as much havoc as a reserve deployment near the door.

The last jumper in the stick then turns around so that the jumper in front can make sure he isn't going to hang himself or spill his rigging lines in intestine-like coils all over the passage way. He turns back and yells "Thirty-two OK" and slaps the jumper in front on the shoulder who in turn repeats "Thirty-one OK" and all the jumpers count-down back to the jumper nearest the door, who shouts, "One OK, stick OK" with a thumbs-up to the dispatchers.

At this point, those jumpers near the door can see Africa rushing by a few feet under the plane. The view is distorted by the waves of hot air from the big Allison turboprop engines of the C-130 or, in the case of the Transall C-160, Rolls Royce turboprops. The trees and bush shimmer in the hazy slipstream and the sweetish smell of burned avtur wafts into the cabin making those prone to nausea just a little sicker. Wind deflectors in front of the doors have been extended, so little fresh air gets in as the pilot throttles back in increments, making the drone of the engines less strident and the vertical bumps less sharp. The hiss and clunk of flaps being lowered, deflectors deployed and all the other last-minute adjustments make the interior sound like a steam laundry.

The command, "Action stations", which always sounds a little over-dramatic on training jumps, today has an authentic ring to it. The chorus, "Action stations", repeated by the paratroopers, is cut short by the beginning of the shuffle-step which bunches everyone up together, with the first pace banging down the heel of the trailing foot on the aluminium floor.

"One, two!"

A red light glows above the door and dispatcher 1 and 2, like hangman's assistants, have a firm grip of the first jumper's harness, keeping him upright and steady a couple of paces from the door. The waiting feels like it will never end; gooseflesh and chilled sweat run in rivulets down the chest under the shirt. Not a sound apart from the droning engines.

08h02: The Canberras get the all clear, turn and head toward Cassinga. Flying at an altitude of 500 feet, they cross the town from north to south and deliver their payloads. Each of the four Canberras drops 300 Alpha anti-personnel bombs, which are small rubber-coated fragmentation bombs, designed to bounce ten metres into the air before detonating. Directly following the Canberras, the Buccaneers approach from the west at low altitude and each delivers its eight 450kg HE bombs onto selected targets. Of the total of thirty-two 1,000lb bombs dropped by the four Buccaneers, 24 score direct hits, causing great damage to buildings. Immediately behind the Buccaneers, the two Mirage III CZs strafe the camp with 30mm HE fragmentation shells. Cassinga becomes masked in dust and smoke as the aircraft head back to base to refuel and re-arm for the second phase of Operation *Reindeer*, the strike on Chetequera (Target Bravo) just north of the South West African–Angolan border.

"Stand in the door!"

"One, two," shuffle-step forward, putting the first jumper with the toe of his front boot out over the lip of the step, his static line thrown toward the rear of the plane, his eyes looking at the horizon.

Just then, the aircraft suddenly pulls upward. This quick climb from treetop height to a jump altitude of 700 feet takes everyone by surprise and the G-forces make everyone instantly much heavier. The only support the paratroopers have is the static line they are hanging onto. Some do a half pirouette, some sink to their knees and most use some really bad language. This sharp pull-up is due to two things. Firstly, Brigadier du Plessis has changed the initial point—IP, the point at which the green light is switched on to initiate the exit—from a road to a path through the bush. He has done this without consulting the commander, Jan Breytenbach, and has only told the pilots. The pilots naturally assume that the change of orders has originated with Colonel Breytenbach. The problem with this changed IP is that the path was clearly visible on the aerial photos but those photos were taken in winter when the bush was thin and the trees had no foliage. Colonel Breytenbach, very experienced in the Angolan bush, knew this and had stipulated a more visible road as the IP. The path is now, at the end of summer, completely overgrown and invisible. The second problem is that the photos, while not only out of date, are incorrectly scaled, showing all the DZs as double the size they actually are. The effect of these two errors is that when the pilots reach their pull-up points, they are actually almost over their IPs so they pull up very quickly and almost simultaneously switch on the green light to commence the drop. This causes a certain amount of chaos inside the aircraft with the heavily laden paratroopers suddenly doubling their weight, just as they are expected to exit.

08h02–08h10: The Hercules and Transall aircraft carrying the paratroopers have started their low altitude formation run toward Cassinga. Inside, the men are given the command "Action stations!" At the last moment, the transports suddenly climb to drop-height (600–800 feet) and almost immediately begin dropping the paratroopers.

The green light above the twin doors of the aircraft blinks on.

"Go!" shouts the dispatcher, simultaneously clouting the jumper in the door on his shoulder. "One, two!" chant the paratroopers, shuffle-stepping doorward.

"Go!" and another jumper disappears from view as if plucked from the door by an invisible hand.

The first few paratroopers out the door were not the elegant stream that training encouraged, but a tumbling, jostling, concertina-like line of a swaying beast of burden. Because of the scaling error, the drop zone was not just half its anticipated length, but also half its width, which caused the pilots huge difficulties. The attacking companies were dropped from three aircraft flying in a V formation roughly north–south between Cassinga base and the river. Because the drop zone was so narrow, the aircraft flying on the left found itself almost over the western edge of the base and the aircraft on the right was forced to edge over the river. Both these enforced options were a problem. On the one hand, paratroopers would find themselves dropped right onto the enemy with no time to form up or regroup before going into battle, and on the other side, paratroopers would find themselves dropped onto the wrong side of the bridgeless river, isolating them from their attack positions.

What was worse, as the pilots reached the end of their unexpectedly shortened drop zones, they found that their aircraft were still half full of paratroopers. The manual dictated that the red light should immediately be switched on to abort the jump, but this would have left only half the attacking force to execute a task already seriously undermanned because of the lack of sufficient helicopters to withdraw the troops. The pilots decided to allow the remaining paratroopers to complete their jump even though they would miss their designated landing areas by considerable margins.

To compound the pilots' problems, the left-hand aircraft was forced to fly over the base itself, exposing it to almost point-blank anti-aircraft gunfire. The right-hand aircraft was being pushed over the river and was forced to drop its paratroopers on the wrong side of this formidable water feature.

Thus the venerable airborne tradition of dropping troops in the wrong place was perpetuated at Cassinga.

Apart from his regular job as a rifleman in one of the two attack companies, the author was tasked with carrying the company medical kit as well as acting as official photographer for the duration of the battle. Colonel Breytenbach had discovered that he was a cameraman by profession, so had loaded him up with a 35mm still camera and a 16mm movie camera to enable him to record events for posterity. Apart from these two army cameras, he also, in contravention of many standing orders, took along his own 35mm still camera to record events for his own edification, plus a pocket-load of fast-speed colour film for his own camera and a few rolls of army-issue monochrome film for the army still camera, as well as a couple of rolls of 16mm film for the army movie camera. There was another still cameraman, Sergeant Des Steenkamp, who also had an army 35mm camera. Steenkamp was appointed in the usual precautionary 'belts and braces' manner in case the author was incapacitated in any way during the battle.

The plan between Steenkamp and the author was that the author would concentrate on filming the whole jump on the movie camera and Steenkamp would snap off some still shots during the jump. Steenkamp used his auto-wind still camera with which to do this. The author was to roll the movie camera, strapped above his reserve, on the command "Go!" to the first jumper. Both Steenkamp and the author had cameras strapped to their reserves, so that in the event of a main parachute malfunction, they would have recorded their deaths by impact with the ground—Steenkamp in single frame, and the author in glorious Technicolor moving images.

The author was not far from the port door as he was number seven in his stick, so in peering sideways he could catch a glimpse of the air force bombing run on the base, due to finish a minute before jumping commenced.

Only dull thuds could be heard above the monotonous drone of the engines as the bombing commenced but visually the results were spectacular. Because of the soft sand upon which the town was built, the bombs sunk well into the ground before exploding. This made the bombing militarily ineffective on the one hand but visually spectacular on the other. Huge, towering geysers of sand and dust were projectile-spewed upward, looking like a chain of volcanoes erupting sequentially along the long line of the bombing axis. But this great cloud of smoke, dust and debris drifting with the brisk morning breeze contributed to the difficulty pilots had in identifying their drop points. Not only was the DZ half the size it was thought to be because of the mistake in scaling, much of the landscape was obscured as well. The brigadier's interference had also exacerbated matters, with the jump already compromised and in some disarray.

The author's personal account of the jump follows:

> I roll my movie camera to film the interior of the plane which at this stage seems for all the world like the chute in a wildebeest game capture.
>
> The sounds of the chanting paratroopers mixed with the shouting dispatchers, the curses of stumbling troops caught up in seat webbing and the controlled chaos of the rapid mass exit combine to resemble the dark, bulky bodies of bucking, snorting animals. Rifle barrels sticking up next to rounded helmets look like a forest of horns cavorting toward the apparent freedom of the open doors.
>
> Before I can think, I am at the door in a flat-out canter. The dispatchers have given up the idea of a controlled jump. The lines in the plane have concertinaed, leaving gaps that are closed by paratroopers running instead of shuffling. I run out of the door, snapping my feet together and tucking my arms in as far as my cameras will allow. The windblast violently pushes into my back allowing me to ride the big air-slide down past the tail. My canopy at full line-stretch has been pushed by the slipstream straight in front and above me. The canopy flutters and billows for a moment before filling with air and is suddenly whipped behind me. A hard tug brings my heavy steel-helmeted head down, ramming my chin into my chest. The parachute has opened. I look up to check that all is fine with the canopy, then have a quick look around to make sure I am not too close to anyone else in the air.
>
> All clear, so I begin panning the movie camera around, getting the bombed town, the dust and smoke plumes and ... "*Porca miseria!* ... What the hell is that?"
>
> A sound unlike anything I have ever heard rips the sky apart. An offbeat, eccentric cyclic stuttering roar like God shouting shatters the relative calm of my parachute descent. We find out later that it was a 14.5mm anti-aircraft gun but at that moment it is a totally unknown factor. The supersonic cracks of the bigger-than-half-inch bullets going past at a high cyclic rate of fire turn guts to water. I cannot see where it is coming from but, turning around to take a still shot with the 35mm camera of the departing aircraft, I can now see the rounds of tracer going away from me in long, shallow arcs. One or two of the rounds penetrate my canopy way above me, leaving neat little heat-sealed holes in their wake. They are shooting at us and my rifle is strapped to my side. I quickly undo my bellyband, freeing my rifle for instant use once I land.
>
> Time to tilt the camera down to take in the landing. I see for the first time the river that should have been half a kilometre away drifting beneath me. This is a catastrophe. We shouldn't be anywhere near the river. The mistake in scaling and the slight drift of the aircraft conspires to put me in the water. I climb my left lift-web to attempt to steer my canopy back onto the correct riverbank, the one closest to the town, and at that moment Des clicks the shutter on the camera, capturing my monkey-climbing trick up the lift-web and my loosened chest-strap waving in the breeze. This is all happening in much less time than it takes to tell it. Our exit altitude of about six to seven hundred feet gives an under-canopy time of a maximum of thirty seconds. There is a stiff breeze blowing the canopies over the river and for a moment there is a tough decision to make: run with the wind and definitely land safely but on the wrong side of the river or try to counter the wind and either land in the river or perhaps on the right side. I am quite used to jumping over water at my civilian skydiving club at Donaldson Dam and I know that the wind will usually diminish the lower one sinks, so I take my chances and climb a single lift-web as high as I can to distort the unmodified canopy to its maximum so as to get some drive against the wind.
>
> I manage to halt the drift over the water and reverse it slightly as the riverbank comes up and slaps me violently in the soles of my boots. The next thing that touches the ground is my head, with a ringing bang on the helmet. I look around and see that my canopy is still inflated and inexorably dragging me to the water.
>
> I quickly release a Capewell clip to collapse the canopy and get shakily to my feet. Just then, what appears to be a pile of baggage smashed into the ground next to me moves a bit and gets taller.

It is Pat O'Leary, my section leader. "Jeez Mac, that was a bit nerve wracking" said Pat. "Give us a smoke."

"Pat, you gave up" I say.

Pat gives up smoking every time we go to the bush. What that really means is that he gives up smoking his own and entreats me to keep the supply chain going. I am used to this and this is one of the reasons why, apart from trade, I have ten packets for a planned single day's battle. Relenting, I walk over to Pat, tap out a cigarette from my packet, hand it to him and put one in my own mouth, leaning over to light Pat's with my Zippo. As I light his cigarette it is shot from his mouth. It turns into a ragged stump between his lips like a clown's exploding cigar. I momentarily see his eyes widen before we simultaneously execute back loops away from one another and scramble for cover.

I did not realize it at the time, but my graceless landing damaged the movie camera and although I kept on shooting with it until the film ran out, I didn't realize it was badly damaged until I tried to change film reels. At least I got the jump in the can.

One paratrooper landed in the high trees alongside the river. He found himself suspended about three meters above the ground and being fired upon by an enemy soldier from just a few paces away. Perhaps his swaying in the breeze saved him from being hit by the long burst of automatic fire from the AK-47, or perhaps the excitement of the moment, and the not-negligible recoil of the assault rifle on full automatic made all the rounds miss but his scramble to unfasten his chest strap paid off. Just as the paratrooper brought his weapon to bear, the SWAPO soldier ran out of ammunition. He immediately threw down his weapon and raised his hands but was not quick enough to avoid the paratrooper double-tapping him in stomach and forehead with his folding-butt R1 para rifle. The paratrooper then unclipped one side of his reserve, punched his quick-release box while sitting in his seat strap, pulled the ripcord on the reserve and slid down the rope of rigging lines that spilled from the reserve like the entrails of a slaughtered cow.

Another paratrooper landed in a tree and found himself suspended a few feet above the ground. On releasing himself from his harness, he fell the remaining few feet, only to knock himself out when he hit the ground. His immediate comrades saw what had happened and picked up the unconscious soldier and carried him along throughout the battle. His comrades saw to it that he was evacuated to the HAA and from there he was transported, still out for the count, back to South Africa. The unlucky soldier only woke from his concussed slumber once he reached the safety of 1 Military Hospital at Voortrekkerhoogte in Pretoria. He remembered nothing of the battle apart from the jump.

CHAPTER FIVE: THE ASSAULT BEGINS

With the attack companies, A and B, dropped too late and overly spread out along the line of flight, the attack was in danger of losing momentum. That half of the attack group was on the wrong side of the river made regrouping very difficult. The paratroopers who were on the Cassinga side of the river needed to move back down the line of flight as much as two kilometres in order to re-establish their planned start line. However, they couldn't do this as they would split their force and lose contact in the heavy bush with their comrades who had to find a river crossing in order to link up and move back down the line. Eventually, after about an hour and a half, the two elements reunited and started moving toward the base. Those who had fallen into the river had, in some cases, jettisoned their kit so as not to drown. Dave McVeigh had emerged from the water without his webbing, rifle and helmet and had to re-equip himself from the enemy. Brigadier du Plessis also found himself neck-deep in the river and was helped ashore by a friendly rifleman extending his rifle barrel so as to tow him out of the river. On emerging from the water, the brigadier met up with the Colonel Jan Breytenbach's radio operator and commandeered him and his radio. This left Colonel Breytenbach without a means of communication with Commandant Archie Moore in the spotter plane and without contact with the operations headquarters in South West Africa.

Lieutenant Jim Harwood, an A Company platoon commander, landed on the wrong side of the river. As soon as he landed, he made contact with some other lost paras similarly misplaced. Harwood received a harrowing radio message from one of his section leaders who was on the correct, or enemy, side of the river. This section leader had linked up with some B Company troops and had come across Eddie Backhouse who had been shot in the chest. Backhouse was in a very bad way and the section leader was urgently requesting a medic. It seems that Backhouse was shot either while still suspended under his parachute or on landing. He had taken an AK-47 round in the centre of his chest, tearing the aorta. Harwood felt totally helpless. He was on the wrong side of a deep, fast-flowing river. He didn't know where the rest of his platoon was and he didn't know where to find a medic to assist Backhouse. Once a medic did eventually get to Backhouse, he was dead.

Colonel Breytenbach, although deprived of his main radio, did have the radio he had jumped with, so he could make contact with his troops on the ground. On the far side of the base, C Company

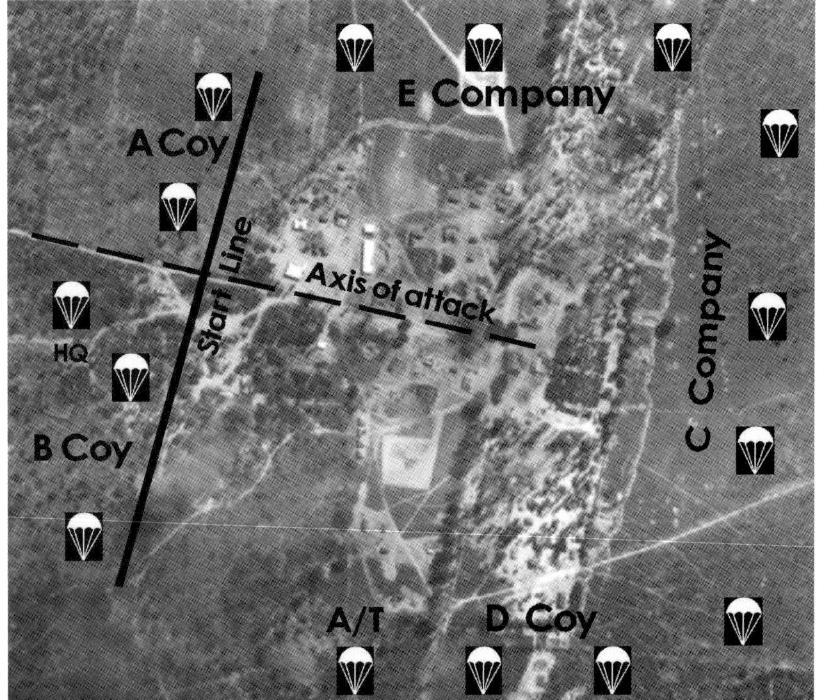

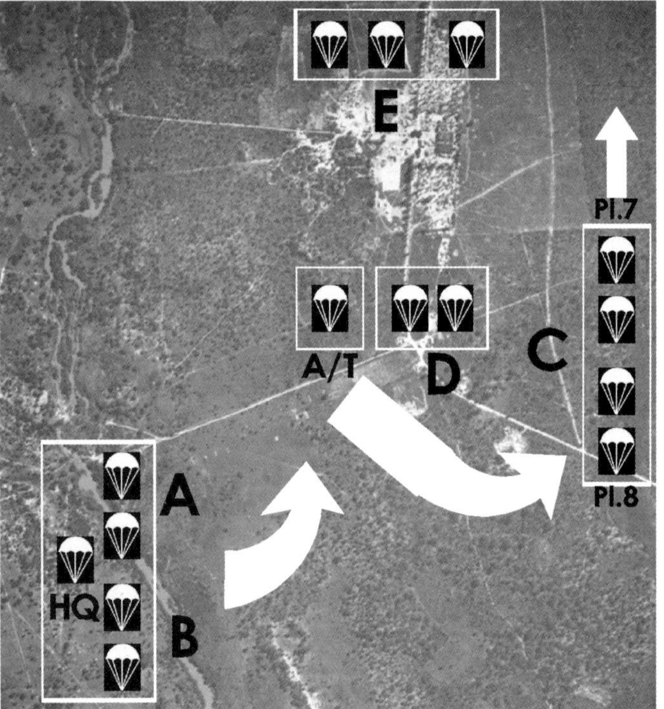

Cassinga: the plan of attack (top) and the actual attack (above).

had also exited their aircraft a few seconds late. This displaced them considerably and they found themselves spread across the road to Techamutete, in high trees and thick bush. They also immediately came into contact with SWAPO troops fleeing the area and sporadic but fierce firefights erupted all along their line. They found it difficult to regroup in the thick bush while busy with firefights, so they only reached their designated stopper group positions about an hour and a half after the jump. This misplacement of both the attack companies, A and B, as well as the stopper groups of C Company allowed the enemy to gather their wits with many escaping the deadly box-drop surrounding them.

It was at this time that the SWAPO chief deserted his command; Dimo Amaambo, military commander of SWAPO in southern Angola, took to his jeep and fled the scene, leaving his troops leaderless to face an assault by some of South Africa's most fearsome soldiers.

Meanwhile, the two independent platoons, 9 Platoon, comprising national servicemen from 1 Parachute Battalion, and 42 Platoon landed almost on target. Of course, their landing was also affected by the scaling error, so 42 Platoon, instead of landing a few hundred meters from the Recruits' Camp, landed right on top of it. This put them into battle immediately and about 50 SWAPO cadres were killed in the short but intense firefight that erupted on landing. These two platoons quickly moved into their planned positions on high ground along the riverbank and were very effective in preventing SWAPO soldiers from fleeing across the river to the northwest.

Cassinga was the first time that paratroopers had come face to face with SWAPO in a pitched battle with no quarter given. Up until now, contact with SWAPO had been restricted to follow-up Reaction Force or Fire Force operations against roving bands of SWAPO in South West Africa. These operations were very often a mismatch in manpower because the paratroopers operated in small *valks* ('falcons', i.e. sticks) of a Puma helicopter carrying-capacity size, with groups of ten paratroopers chasing down much larger groups of up to 30 SWAPO guerrillas. While the fighting capability of the SWAPO soldiers was never discounted, their tactics were to strike at soft civilian targets and then run for the border, at all times trying to avoid contact with the South Africans. As a result the paratroopers were accustomed to SWAPO fleeing rather than making a stand.

Cassinga was different. Because of the box-drop around the base, SWAPO had nowhere to run and they rose to the challenge. Sun Tzu, the Chinese military strategist spoke of the Golden Bridge one should offer the enemy if a quick victory was needed. This means that if a real or apparent route to safety were offered to a besieged enemy, he would naturally use it, thus making the attacker's task much easier. The opposite of course applies. If no route to safety is offered, the enemy has no choice but to fight to the death defending his ground. This is what happened at Cassinga. Colonel Breytenbach had learned many years previously, while on a course at Fort Benning in the USA that the dictum, "Find 'em, fix 'em and finish 'em" was the key to the success of an airborne attack. The air force photo interpreters had 'found' Fortress Cassinga, the bombers and box-drop of paratroopers had 'fixed' the enemy in place, and now the attacking companies were going to 'finish 'em' by either sweeping through their defences from the unexpected river side and shooting them in their trenches, or by driving them into the stopper groups surrounding the base.

D Company on the southern side of the base was misplaced by 500 metres and when converging on the Engineering Complex encountered some of the misplaced B and C company troops; only good fire discipline prevented any friendly-fire casualties. One D Company paratrooper was injured when his section came

A Company approaching the fortifications

SWAPO dead in the trenches

Captured Eastern bloc small arms.

under RPG fire and some ammunition dumps began exploding in the buildings around them. D Company quickly suppressed all opposition and took up their positions as stoppers while the Anti-Tank Platoon was sent to lay a pattern of mines on the Techamutete road to prevent the Cubans from coming to SWAPO's rescue, should the battle drag on. This foresight in planning was to be a saving grace later in the day.

Seeing the complete misplacement of his attack group, Colonel Breytenbach sensed that the element of surprise had been lost because of the time taken to regroup. He made the brave decision to alter his axis of attack and instead of spending another half hour marching back to the planned positions he formed the attack companies A and B up at 90° to their planned axis and signalled to immediately commence the attack. The services of Commandant Archie Moore in the light Cessna 185 spotter aircraft would have been of great value during this repositioning of paratroopers; however, it had been forced away by the heavy fire from the anti-aircraft guns.

Paratroopers under heavy fire during the advance.

CHAPTER SIX: THE BATTLE

The Canberra and Buccaneer bombers had meanwhile left for Ondangwa and Grootfontein to refuel and re-arm for the attack on the second target, Chetequera. This series of small bases was to be attacked by an armoured force supported by bombers. Because of the regrouping delays at Cassinga, the enemy there had time to organize themselves into a formidable defensive force.

At Cassinga, those who had not been affected by the bombing took up defensive positions in the trenches and buildings of the base. A lone Buccaneer, armed with six dozen SNEB rockets, circled the base, giving the paratroopers close air support where needed. The SWAPO defenders were armed with the full gamut of the Soviet arsenal: 14.5 heavy machine guns, RPG rocket launchers, B10 recoilless rifles, 82mm mortars, RPD machine guns, SKS rifles, AK-47 assault rifles, PPSh sub-machine guns, pistols and grenades. From bunkers, buildings and trenches all were being used against the paratroopers in a storm of fire which had the attackers leopard-crawling much of the way toward the camp. The base was surrounded by fairly thick bush, apart from a millet field at one end, so the attackers had no idea how far they were from the trenches at any time. The fire-and-movement method of advance was being used whenever any resistance was encountered. While one side of the skirmish line took cover and laid down covering fire the other advanced in a series of dashes. After each dash, the alternate side began laying down covering fire so as to allow their other wing to catch up and straighten the line. This covering fire was directed low into bushes whence the enemy might be shooting and at the left-hand-side bases of trees from where right-handed guerrillas might be shooting.

One of the difficulties with the advance was the unsanitary nature of the area. It became clear to the paratroopers that the camp had few, if any, latrines. The bush around the camp was covered with human excrement, which made diving for cover a challenging business. The paratroopers, with disregard for their safety, took to running a little farther or to one side in order to avoid diving into a pile of the foul stuff. Whether this sanitation regime was a deliberate policy to obtain more money from UNICEF or

AK-47 assault rifle.
Source: Wikicommons

RPG-7 rocket-propelled grenade.
Source: Wikicommons

PPSh sub-machine gun.
Source: Wikicommons

SKS rifles.
Source: Wikicommons

simply indiscipline, is unclear. The SWAPO soldiers at Cassinga had dug an extensive trench and bunker system so digging a few latrines should have been a simple task. UNICEF on the other hand had vast funds available for the improvement of sanitation at refugee camps, so this lack of sanitation may have been part of the greater deception to garner more funds to be redirected toward SWAPO's war effort.

Operation *Reindeer* had not begun very well for Rifleman Dale Packham. He had somehow managed to leave all his kit, together with his ammunition and rifle behind at Bloemspruit AFB. This, in a paratrooper's world, was the worst possible offence a trooper could commit. When Packham's platoon sergeant reported the sin to Hugo Murray, the commander of B Company, he summoned the rifleman and gave him the bad news: not only was Packham the world's worst soldier but he was going to be left behind. This was a fate worse than anything Packham could imagine. After all the hard work, sweat and suffering, he was reduced to tears by Murray's disciplinary punishment. Packham begged to be allowed to go with his comrades and Murray grudgingly agreed to let this happen so long as Packham could be fully kitted out, replacing his missing jump helmet, his webbing, weapon, ammunition, rations and water. Packham's platoon sergeant promised to rectify the situation. Within two hours, the sergeant had somehow scrounged all the missing gear from somewhere, including an R1 paratrooper's folding-stock rifle which should have been unavailable anywhere in Grootfontein.

Things would get worse for Packham before they got better. 'Stony' Steenkamp was having a torrid time trying to find a crossing point on the river in order to join his company, Hugo Murray's B Company. Among the troops with Steenkamp were an LMG gunner, van Vuuren and his buddy Anthony Modena. Van Vuuren had lost his LMG barrel so was effectively disarmed. This motley crew eventually managed to join Murray who welcomed the relatively fresh platoon and ordered them to attack two machine guns in a trench position that had A Company pinned down. They were ordered to proceed through some buildings which were on one side of the road that designated the axis of attack. After a swift firefight, they captured the buildings then used them as a firebase to pour a heavy volume of fire at the anti-aircraft guns in the strongpoint which were proving problematic for the attack companies. However, attempts by the platoon to halt the heavy machine-gun fire failed and it too found itself pinned down.

Steenkamp had, in the meantime, picked up more lost paras which brought his platoon up to a slightly over-strength situation. Warrant Officer Norman Reeves who had joined him and had helped in taking the buildings was then wounded in the chest when a stray round struck a pencil-flare launcher in his pocket. At the same time, Rifleman Koelman was hit in the neck. Packham and several others rushed to their aid.

Leaving his buddies to drag the wounded pair to safety, Packham decided to single-handedly take on the machine guns that were

MiG-19. *Source: Wikicommons*

MiG-21s flying in formation. *Source: Wikicommons*

Paras sweep through the vehicle park.

These paratroopers have just finished clearing one of the hundreds of trenches.

causing all the trouble. He charged round the corner of the building into the combined fire of the 14.5mm and 32mm heavy machine guns. Inevitably he was hit, in the arm and chest, and was knocked down. A devastatingly powerful 14.5mm bullet left him dazed and in great pain. He lay out in the open while heavy rounds kicked up dust around him.

Murray then received a message telling him that a paratrooper had been badly wounded. He had just seen Norman Reeves on his feet at the aid station, so knew it wasn't Reeves who was seriously wounded. Realizing it was a fresh casualty, he ordered Rifleman Deville Engelbrecht, the company medic, to go to the wounded paratrooper's aid. Engelbrecht set off at speed, covering 60 metres of bullet-swept ground to get to the wounded man who was lying in the open with bullets kicking up showers of stones and sand all about him. Engelbrecht crawled up to the wounded soldier and tried to take his pulse but found that shock had stiffened his muscles and it was impossible to feel a pulse, let alone find a vein into which a drip could be inserted. Both soldiers were now under increasingly heavy fire and Engelbrecht knew that it was only a matter of time before both of them would be hit. He had to get Packham into cover in order to treat his very serious condition. Engelbrecht then positioned himself on his backside,

More SWAPO dead in a trench.

Captured communist weaponry.

The SWAPO communications centre is destroyed.

behind Packham, pulled the wounded man up into his lap and started shuffling backward to the shelter of the nearest building. Inch by inch, the pair made their laborious way back to cover and out of the heavy machine guns' arcs of fire. Once in cover, Engelbrecht found that he still couldn't find a vein for a drip but he did manage to inject Packham with a vial of the painkiller Sosegon.

Having done what he could for Packham, Engelbrecht decided to report to Murray and get help in moving Packham to the Regimental Aid Post, the RAP. He retraced his steps to his company commander, sprinting the 60 deadly metres back to where he had started. When he told Murray that the wounded soldier had taken a round in the neck and then in his chest cavity and was coughing blood, a worried Murray inquired who the soldier was. Engelbrecht told him it was Dale Packham, the same soldier Murray had torn a strip off for leaving his kit at Bloemspruit. When Murray asked whether Packham would live, Engelbrecht replied that he didn't know but felt he had had to return and tell Murray because the platoon radio was out of action.

Colonel Breytenbach had in his HQ two doctors, Rassie Tauscher and Chris George, who were better qualified than Engelbrecht to render treatment to the badly wounded Packham. Murray broke into Breytenbach's command net to request urgent medical help for Packham who would soon die without it. Murray was unaware

SWAPO barracks burn, with the body of a uniformed guerrilla in the foreground. The large tree on the right, also burning, had housed several SWAPO snipers who were eventually dealt with.

A view over the trenches toward the parade ground.

Captured SWAPO wounded. Contrary to SWAPO propaganda, captured guerrillas were treated humanely; paras were under strict orders not to shoot captures out of hand.

that both doctors had lost most of their kit when landing in the river. The colonel immediately dispatched both doctors to their as-yet-established RAP where they eventually met up with Engelbrecht who escorted them to Murray's HQ. There they waited while Engelbrecht again risked his life by traversing the 60 metres of open, bullet-swept ground to the hut where he had left Packham who was now delirious. The exhausted medic gathered Packham up in his arms, knowing that the traditional fireman's carry would cause untold damage to Packham's chest wound. For the fourth time he took a slow trot back through the hail of bullets for the longest 60 metres of his life, to safety, where the doctors were able to stabilize the wounded man. (Both Packham, who survived his wounds, and Engelbrecht were subsequently awarded the Honoris Crux. Colonel Breytenbach said later that Engelbrecht should have been awarded the Honoris Crux Silver but one eyewitness report was so self-serving that it ruined the chance for the deserving medic.)

Next, A Company moved through the camp's vehicle park with its collection of olive-drab Soviet Gaz trucks and troop carriers whence there was heavy return fire from SWAPO. Some of the enemy were firing from the cover of the big steel wheels of the trucks. This situation was to prove the benefits of the full-bore NATO 7.62mm round the paratroopers used in their folding-butt R1 rifles. Where the enemy presumed he was safe from return fire behind a steel wheel, he was neutralized by the paratroopers shooting straight through the tyre and the rim. Another vantage point for the enemy was a bus that had been hijacked from South West Africa with children and civilians on board and had been driven to Cassinga a few weeks earlier so that the passengers could be paraded as refugees to the UNHCR inspection team visiting the base. Many of the defenders had climbed on board the bus, either to effect their escape, or because it was a good position from which to direct fire onto the paratroopers. Every few seconds, a guerrilla would pop up at one of the windows and take a shot at the advancing paratroopers. Lieutenant Dolf du Plessis told his LMG

Uniformed PLAN troops as prisoners of war on the parade ground.

gunner to rake the sides of the bus with long bursts of fire. Every time the LMG stopped firing two or three guerrillas would dash from the door of the bus only to be cut down by para riflemen. This continued until there was a large pile of bodies outside the door of the bus. The rest of the guerrillas in the bus eventually decided that they were trapped and surrendered by throwing their weapons from the windows and trooping out the door, stepping gingerly over their dead comrades to join the growing crowd of prisoners near the parade ground.

Slowly, the momentum of the attack was regained. Where the attack companies had had to take cover under withering fire for minutes at a time, now as the fighting neared the trenches, the paratroopers were able to move upright and at a run during lulls in the barrage. Johan Blaauw and 9 Platoon were now attacking the housing where the Cuban instructors were presumed to live.

09h30: The Buccaneer, armed with 72 68mm SNEB rockets, arrives from Grootfontein. Without first consulting the battalion commander, the Forward Air Control (FAC) clears the Buccaneer to strike the buildings north of Cassinga. Unbeknown to the FAC and the pilot, 9 Platoon has already started clearing the buildings. The Buccaneer dispatches 39 rockets into the buildings. Although some soldiers from 9 Platoon are wounded, there are no fatalities. The Buccaneer is called off immediately.

9 Platoon was meant to be supported in this attack by the Mortar Platoon who, because of the misplaced drop, found themselves beyond effective range to offer supporting fire. The commander of 9 Platoon decided to press his attack, despite the lack of supporting fire from the mortars. The small spotter aircraft, still in the vicinity, reported over the radio that the mortar rounds were falling far short of the target. The Buccaneer pilot then decided to rocket the buildings instead, not realizing that the paratroopers were already house-clearing in and among the buildings. Two paratroopers were wounded by the rocket attack before it was frantically called off over the radio.

Throughout the attack, the enemy 14.5 anti-aircraft guns were a great threat. Used in a ground role these guns had awesome firepower and were being manned by some very courageous SWAPO gunners. Time and again the guns were silenced by paratrooper firepower but started up within minutes with replacement SWAPO soldiers stepping into the breach. In one incident, a frustrated paratrooper took the drastic step of climbing a tree in order to spot for the 60mm mortar teams in an effort to neutralize the guns. Sergeant Verster directed fire onto one anti-aircraft gun by shouting directions to the hand-held mortar beneath his tree. The first rounds were smoke shells because the gun was very close to the forward line of attacking paratroopers and a hand-held mortar is not the most accurate weapon in the

Paras with a captured recoilless rifle.

hands of soldiers under intense fire. The first smoke round scored a bull's eye, giving the SWAPO gunners something to cough over. The next few rounds were close but not close enough. The gun was eventually silenced by a direct hit from the store of rapidly dwindling mortar rounds carried by the paratroopers.

The author, trying to get a photograph of one of the 14.5 anti-aircraft guns, was at one stage startled by a rattling sound from the tree directly above him. A mortar round had tossed a human spine with ribs attached high into the air. The sound was of the bones, picked clean by the high explosive, rattling through the branches.

Once the paratroopers of A and B companies entered the base itself, they came under heavy sniper fire from the many trees dotted around the camp. Heavy fire from anti-tank recoilless B10s was also experienced as well as small-arms fire coming from those trenches which had not as yet been overrun. Paratrooper Mark Kaplan was mortally injured during this time. Hit by a bullet in the chest, he died before his comrades could get to him. The remaining SWAPO soldiers were now being concentrated in the northern part of the base. They still retained much of their firepower and, because of their geographical concentration, could be led in a far more effective manner than a force scattered around the base.

Whoever had taken over the command of the defenders after Dimo Amaambo had fled was doing an admirable job. A SWAPO report written after the battle, the Nayemba Report, noted that SWAPO cadres numbering about 600, half of which had just returned from the Hainyeko Training Centre began "retaliating very bravely".

With one of the 14.5 anti-aircraft guns neutralized, there were still two more to go. Placed in a rough triangle within the base perimeter, these guns managed to pin down the attacking force for some considerable time. The paratroopers were also coming under sniper fire which, in almost a spotting role, seemed to be directing the anti-aircraft guns onto them. B Company was brought to a complete halt by the combined fire of two of these heavy weapons. The guns were temporarily silenced many times, only to start up again when SWAPO dragged the dead and wounded gunners away to be replaced with fresh troops. This speaks highly of the level of training SWAPO had undergone. Many, if not all, seemed capable and willing to take over as heavy machine-gunners when their comrades were killed. The substitute gunners knew enough about the guns to keep up a very effective, continuous barrage for many hours. The fact that the surviving SWAPO soldiers knew that there was no escape from the attacking paratroopers or their stopper groups lent them greater resolve in their defence. The paratroopers needed to maintain their momentum or be bogged down by the heavy machine guns until nightfall or until the Cubans at Techamutete roused themselves to come and help their allies.

With this in mind Colonel Breytenbach ordered Captain Tommie Lamprecht to take the anti-aircraft gun causing the most damage. Lamprecht was resigned to the fact that Alpha and Bravo companies were getting all the action and that his company was, in effect, Colonel Breytenbach's reserve as they had completed their task and were now twiddling their thumbs.

Hearing that the attack companies were pinned down by the AA guns, he called the colonel to remind him that he was available to help. He took around 20 of his men through the vehicle park to begin attacking up the line of trenches leading to the AA gun. He formed his men up but came under heavy fire, so had to re-form in a safer position. He took half his men and went to the right of the trenches with Staff Sergeant Sampie Stoffberg taking the left. Both started the attack by hurling HE and white phosphorus grenades into the nearest trenches and shooting those SWAPO who emerged, some burning brightly with the impossible-to-extinguish phosphorus.

After advancing up the trench line, Lamprecht found that some of his men had lagged behind, so he sent Stoffberg to chivvy them along. Lamprecht then made a rush for the next line of trenches, with Rifleman Kokkie de Waal. As they dashed forward, luck ran out for de Waal. He was hit and stumbled. Seeing this, Lamprecht fell on top of him, rolling him behind the meagre cover of a small tree. The 14.5 AA gun now had a target and although shooting a little high, prevented the two men from moving. At the other end of the trenches Sampie Stoffberg had also been wounded, severely, and was unable to help. Lamprecht noticed that Corporal van der Merwe was pinned down in open ground just to his rear. He asked him to throw a grenade into the trench where the fire was coming from but van der Merwe was unable to raise his head, let alone come to his knees to throw a grenade. Lamprecht had no choice but to rely on his own resources. Pulling a grenade from his kidney pouch, he threw it at the trench but neglected to pull the pin. This silly act served to galvanize him. He looked around to see that his signaller, Corporal Petzer, had on his own initiative found a relatively sheltered spot in the buildings behind Lamprecht and was laying down supporting fire. Lamprecht picked up the unresponsive de Waal and dashed across the open ground to the buildings with bullets kicking up dust around his heels. On reaching the shelter of the buildings, he found that de Waal had died of his wounds. He left his body with Petzer and some B Company troops who had turned up and returned to the fray.

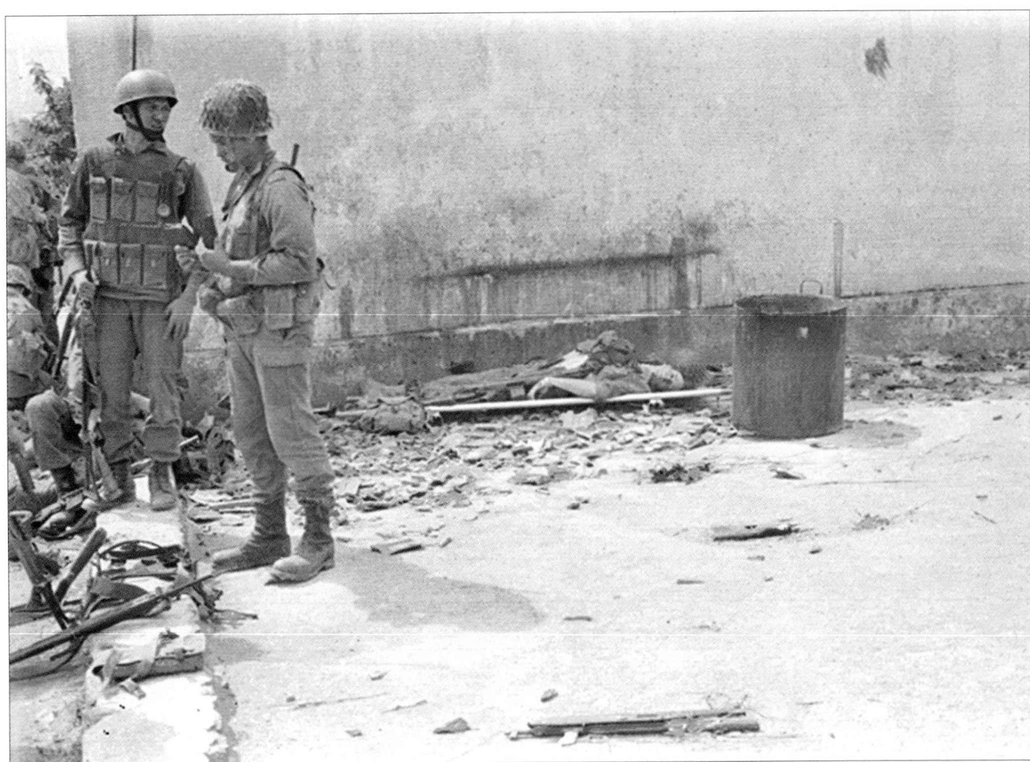

A dead paratrooper in the Field Hospital area.

Colonel Breytenbach then brought every available mortar onto the target and started hammering the AA gun. Breytenbach still had some RPG rounds at his disposal but by now had heard that these might well be needed to neutralize the approaching armoured column from Techamutete that had been reported by the circling Buccaneer. The Mortar Platoon as well as every available patrol mortar pounded the position while Lamprecht and Corporal van der Merwe entered the trenches and went from trench to trench, killing the occupants on their way to the big gun. With rifle and grenade, Lamprecht and van der Merwe wiped out all resistance.

Some people dressed in civilian clothes were in the outlying trenches and it was unclear to Lamprecht whether they were being used as human shields or whether they were combatants out of uniform as SWAPO often were. As they neared the big gun, the defenders were all dressed in uniform, with some women soldiers who fought back fiercely. The trenches were narrow, barely allowing two people to squeeze past one another, so fighting in the zigzag pattern was a kill-or-be-killed enterprise. There was no time to demand surrender or hold fire. Every time Lamprecht or van der Merwe turned a corner a new scene presented itself. Sometimes the enemy were shooting at the paratroopers outside the trench system, oblivious of the danger approaching from within; at others a face-to-face confrontation resulted in the quickest on the trigger living and the slower dying.

Lamprecht and van der Merwe developed an effective way of dealing with the enemy. If one of them was immobilized by enemy fire, the other would expose himself momentarily to draw fire while the other shot at whoever was trying to eliminate his buddy. Each trench comprised three or four zigs and zags, each straight length about three or four metres long and about one and a half metres deep. The noise was indescribable: a deafening mix of the slurred explosions of the big guns and the staccato crackle of small-arms fire, mostly the tenor tones of AK-47s and the lighter chatter of PPSh sub-machine guns, punctuated with the whooshing roars of RPG and B10 rounds. This cacophony was underlaid with the paratroopers' battle talk, the yelling of the enemy and the uncontrolled cooking off of ammunition dumps spread around the base. Finally, Lamprecht and van der Merwe killed the last reserves manning the AA gun and it was stilled for the rest of the day. (Van der Merwe was awarded the Honoris Crux for his sustained bravery that day. Because Lamprecht's actions were largely unwitnessed by a superior, he did not receive what Colonel Breytenbach said should have been an Honoris Crux Silver.)

Lamprecht then took a moment to stick his head above the parapet of the trench, only to be confronted with the barrel of a PPSh sub-machine gun firing at him on full automatic. Fortunately for him, the rounds were all high, going over his head. He raised his rifle to shoot back, only to hear the firing pin click. He had run out of ammunition. He dropped to his knees in the trench to extract a fresh magazine from his ammunition pouches but was unable

Dead uniformed PLAN soldiers.

to do so due to his cramped position. Johan Blaauw had by this time joined up with Lamprecht's group and one of his men met Lamprecht in his trench. Lamprecht whispered to the paratrooper to "Shoot the bastard".

The trooper, amazed by this diminutive officer, whispered back, "What?"

"Shoot the bastard. There!" whispered Lamprecht, pointing up and over the trench top.

"What?"

By now, Lamprecht had managed to reload his rifle.

"Never mind" he said in a matter-of-fact tone while he came to his feet and double-tapped the SWAPO soldier in the face.

By now Lamprecht had used up most of his ammunition and figured to conserve what was left by getting SWAPO to surrender to him. He shouted to the remaining SWAPO soldiers in the adjoining trenches in English and Afrikaans to surrender immediately. This was not something SWAPO ever did without trying to get out of uniform and pretend they were innocent civilians; the habit stuck, even in a pitched battle. The South Africans were treated to the sight of an apparent wrestling match in the trenches while SWAPO soldiers tried to divest themselves of their incriminating uniforms without exposing themselves to enemy fire. Lamprecht and his men, while waiting for the surrender, took pot shots at the odd head or torso that exposed itself during the disrobing process. After a few long minutes, all those SWAPO who had not been shot emerged with raised hands and in various states of undress. Some had mismatched shoes, shirts inside out and pants falling down due to the absence of belts.

Breytenbach received a strange message from the circling Buccaneer at about this time. The pilot, who was now understandably cautious after his premature rocket attack had wounded some paratroopers, asked the colonel what he should do about a white jeep-type vehicle with a red star on its bonnet that he could see speeding away from the base. The pilot had already asked someone 'higher up' for permission to engage, but had been told to make sure it was "not our own people". The colonel somewhat impatiently told him to destroy it because the paratroopers hadn't jumped with any motorized transport. The Buccaneer pilot gave a relieved acknowledgement and proceeded to shoot up the jeep and its occupants. There is no record as to who these might have been.

Another strange request received by Breytenbach was a radio message from Brigadier du Plessis who was occupying the rear, to report back to him in order to keep him abreast of developments. Naturally the colonel refused and suggested that if the brigadier, a tourist at the battle, wanted to know what was happening at the sharp end, the best way to find out was to come there himself. The brigadier never turned up, preferring, like Gilbert and Sullivan's Duke of Plaza Toro to "lead his regiment from behind, he found it more exciting".

Johan Blaauw was having the time of his life. He had complained to the colonel that he was taking heavy fire from the trenches that A Company should have cleared, had the axis of attack not swung 90 degrees. It was now up to B Company to do the job, but they were pre-occupied with the AA guns. Blaauw took to the job himself, sprinting over 20 metres of bare bullet-swept ground to a large bunker containing a gaggle of SWAPO. He jumped onto the low roof and tossed a couple of grenades into the doorway. Inside, about 20 SWAPO were killed in the confined space. The taking of the trenches was a bloody and traumatic business. Some of the trenches had in them people dressed in civilian clothes, some of whom attempted to climb out of the trenches and surrender to the paratroopers, before being dragged back in by uniformed SWAPO soldiers and used as human shields. Some of these, presumably non-combatants, were unavoidably killed when the paratroopers were shot at by SWAPO soldiers hiding behind them. Some small children luckily survived and were carried to the safety of the field hospital area by concerned paratroopers.

The paratroopers clearing the trenches found how useful their folding-butt R1 rifles could be. The trenches were narrow and jammed with corpses and critically wounded SWAPO, leaving little room to manoeuvre. They found themselves clambering over piles of bodies. Slick with blood and other bodily fluids, the footing was precarious and a full-length rifle would have simply

Practice jump at Pietersburg.

The hangar at Grootfontein, as seen at midnight.

Paras in training, standing by to kit up.
Source: Vlamgat

An iconic photo of the drop. The author is climbing up one of his lift-webs in a desperate attempt to steer his parachute away from the river.

The A Company Leader Group changes the axis of attack.

One of the neutralized 14.5mm anti-aircraft gun positions that effectively kept the paratroopers pinned down for long periods, inflicting some serious casualties. These guns were manned by some very brave SWAPO gunners who fought to the bitter end.

An RAP, a Regimental Aid Post, with wounded paratroopers and a SWAPO guerrilla, seen partially at front left.

Colonel Jan Breytenbach (third from left) confers with some of his senior commanders.

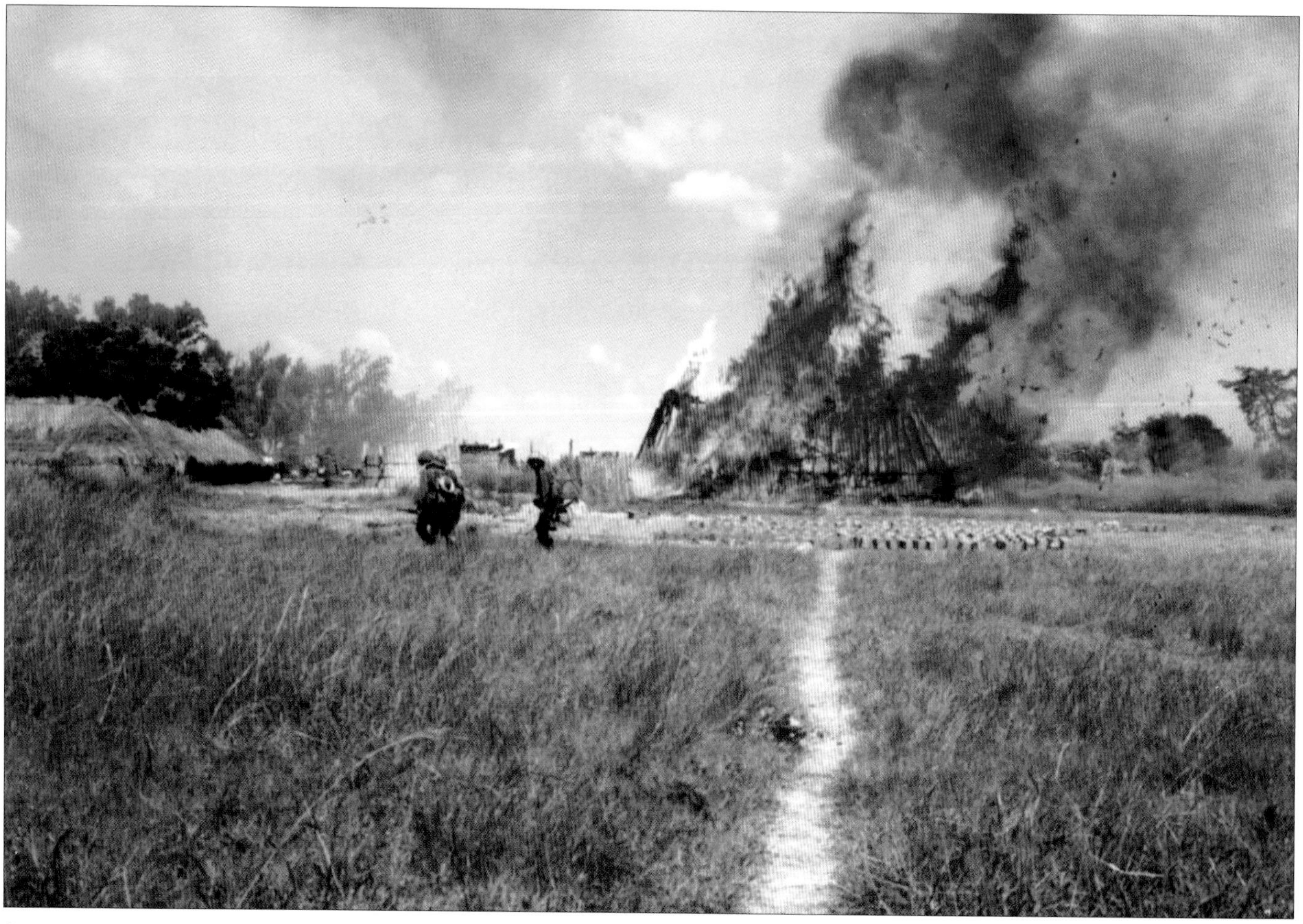

An ammunition dump 'cooks off'. In front, a paratrooper demolition team moves on to its next target.

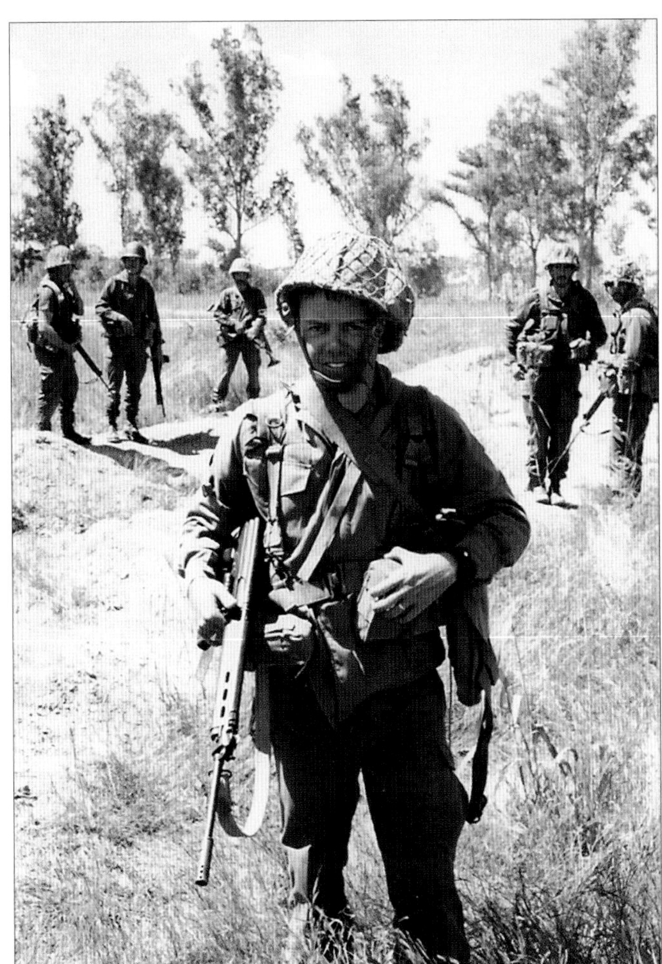

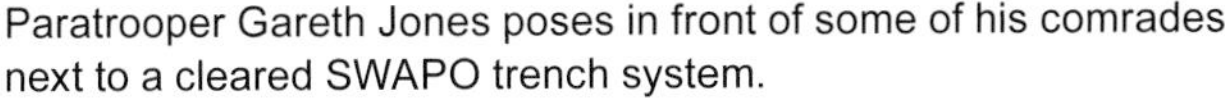

Paratrooper Gareth Jones poses in front of some of his comrades next to a cleared SWAPO trench system.

Paratroopers showing signs of strain. The one in front holds a captured PPSh sub-machine gun.

The ammunition dump reduced to ashes. At extreme right is a para shepherding SWAPO prisoners.

Perhaps fearing for their lives, POWs chant the victors' praises—bizarrely so—no doubt to ingratiate themselves with their captors.

With half the attacking force already evacuated, the remaining paras hurriedly assemble to counter the Cuban/ FAPLA armoured column from Techamutete that is closing in on Cassinga.

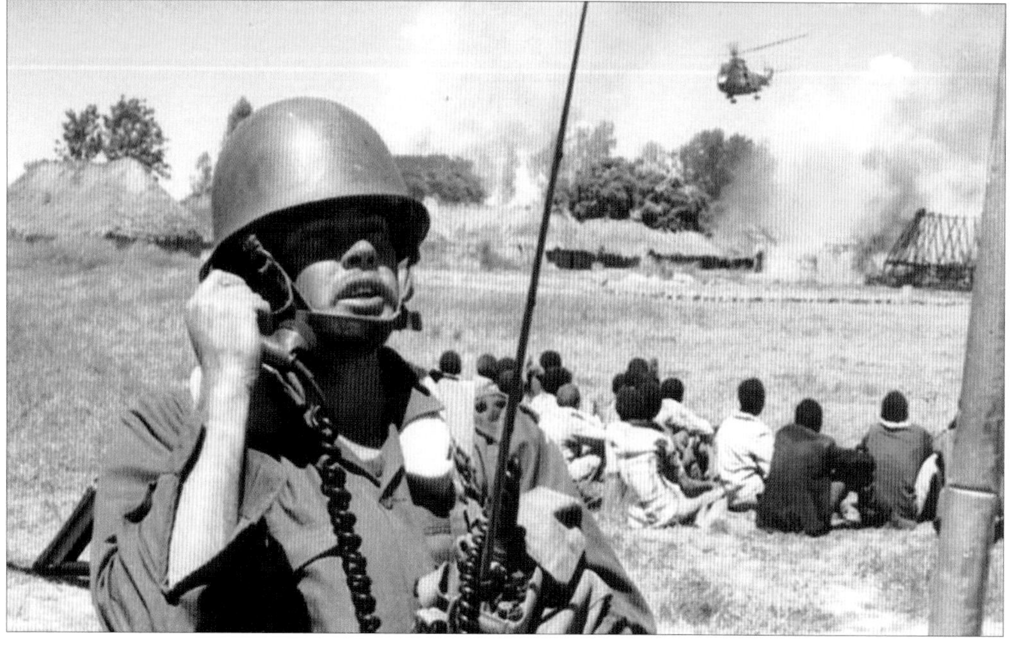
A radio operator directs helicopters into the LZs to start uplifting the troops.

A Puma evacuates troops. The author snapped this photo shortly after he'd been ejected from this particular, overfull helicopter.

Mirage FIII CZ.
Source: From Fledgling to Eagle

Mirage FIII CZ.
Source: From Fledgling to Eagle

Buccaneer
Source: From Fledgling to Eagle

Soviet MiG-19 with armaments. *Source: Wikicommons*

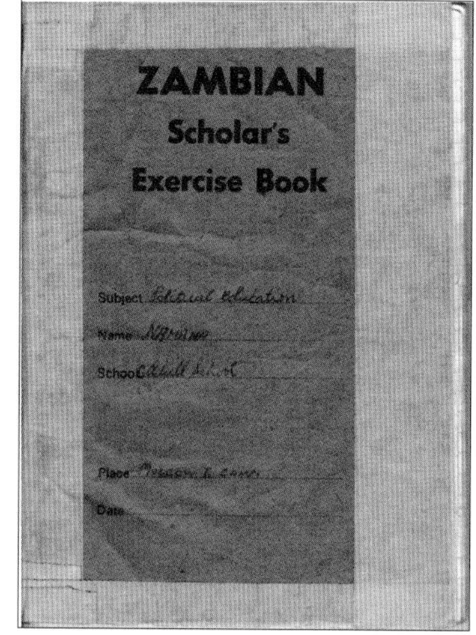
ZAMBIAN
Scholar's
Exercise Book
Subject Political Education
Name
School
Place
Date

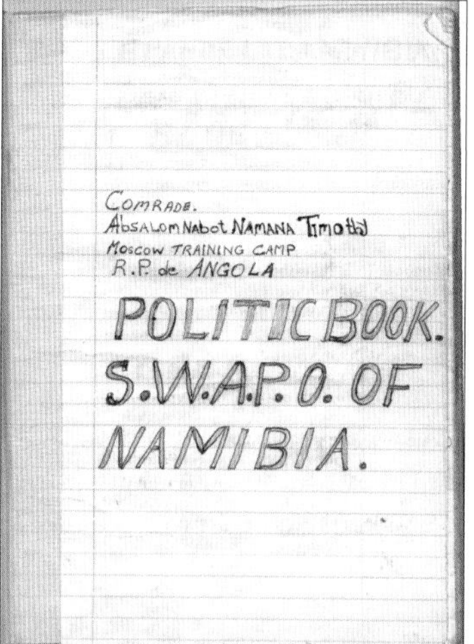
COMRADE.
Absalom Nabot Namana Timothy
Moscow Training Camp
R.P. de ANGOLA
POLITIC BOOK.
S.W.A.P.O. OF
NAMIBIA.

ZU 23-2 dual-barrelled anti-aircraft gun. *Source: Wikicommons*

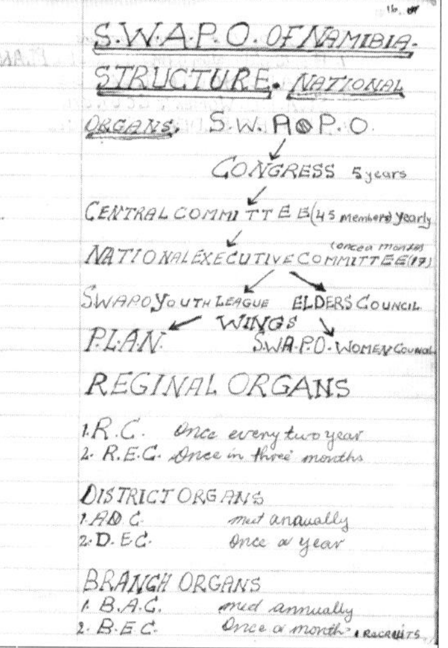
S.W.A.P.O. OF NAMIBIA.
STRUCTURE. NATIONAL
ORGANS. S.W.A.P.O.
CONGRESS 5 years
CENTRAL COMMITTEE (45 members) yearly
NATIONAL EXECUTIVE COMMITTEE (17) (once a months)
SWAPO YOUTH LEAGUE ELDERS COUNCIL
WINGS
P.L.A.N. S.W.A.P.O. WOMEN COUNCIL
REGINAL ORGANS
1. R.C. Once every two year
2. R.E.C. Once in three months
DISTRICT ORGANS
1. A.D.C. met anaually
2. D.E.C. Once a year
BRANCH ORGANS
1. B.A.C. mid annually
2. B.E.C. Once a month · RECRUITS

14.5 anti-aircraft gun.
Source: Wikicommons

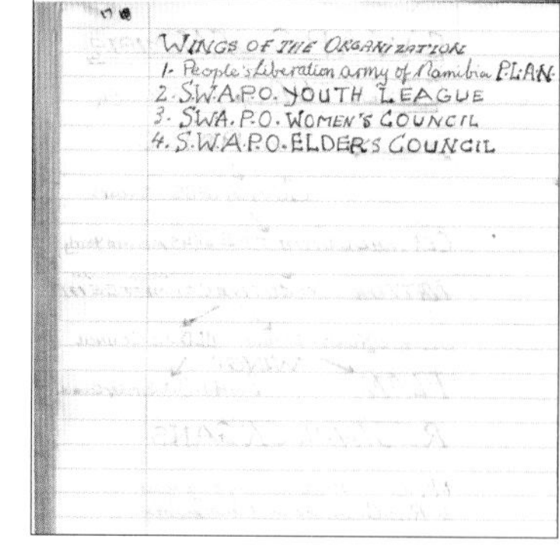
WINGS OF THE ORGANIZATION
1. People's Liberation army of Namibia P.L.A.N.
2. S.W.A.P.O. YOUTH LEAGUE
3. SWA.P.O. WOMEN'S COUNCIL
4. S.W.A.P.O. ELDER'S COUNCIL

The SWAPO/PLAN soldier's notebook, taken from Cassinga by Jan Volschenk.

been unusable in the cramped space. The much-shortened Para-rifle was a boon with the butt folded and proved far quicker to bring to bear than the full-length wooden-butt AK-47s and SKS rifles the enemy were using.

Bernie Fouché was having troubles of a different nature. He had come across a small party of children cowering in the bush. Fouché and his men tried to sooth them with gifts of sweets and Tarzan bars from their meagre rations, even handing over a precious water bottle to the kids who appeared very hungry and thirsty. The children could not speak English but could understand a few words of Afrikaans, so Fouché, with simple words and mimed actions signalled to them to lie down beneath the deadly 14.5 AA gunfire and stay where they were until the battle was over. These children were possibly part of the group kidnapped from St Mary's Mission to masquerade as refugees for the UNICEF inspectors a couple of weeks earlier. Their understanding of Afrikaans, rudimentary as it was, certainly indicated so.

Having killed the snipers harassing them from the trees, B Company had meanwhile turned their attention to the remaining big guns. They directed light machine-gun fire at the gun positions, keeping the gunners' heads down while leopard-crawling paratroopers approached the guns with grenades in hand. The construction of the trench system actually assisted the paratroopers attempting to close with the entrenched defenders. Either because of laziness or inexperience, the trench diggers had left long, shallow piles of excavated earth next to the trenches. This meant that the defenders in the trenches could not keep their fire low because they couldn't depress their weapons sufficiently. This allowed the attacking paratroopers several inches of dead ground, enough to crawl right up to the mounds next to the trenches. From there they could simply roll grenades into the trench and immediately after the resulting explosions get to their feet and fire directly down into the trench.

Eventually, the combined efforts of the mortar men, the light machine-gunners and the trench-clearing teams resulted in the big guns being silenced for the last time. Scattered around the biggest gun, a 23mm ZU 23-2 dual-barrelled anti-aircraft gun, were the bodies of seven defenders and in the surrounding trenches lay the corpses of almost a hundred SWAPO soldiers.

Lieutenant Hans Human and his platoon were pinned down by sniper fire emanating from some very tall, bushy gum trees within the base. The platoon had found cover in the excrement-strewn area on the edge of the base and any slight movement from one of the paratroopers was followed by a fusillade of sniper fire, fortunately not very accurate.

Eventually the paratroopers, weary of the stalemate, agreed on a plan of action. The whole platoon would closely observe the suspected trees while one paratrooper exposed himself to the persistent sniper. As the decoy jumped up, a shot rang out and dislodged a few leaves from the tree. This presented Human's men with the target they were seeking. The entire platoon fired a well-aimed volley at the spot where the leaves had fallen and were rewarded with a rattling sound from the tree as the sniper and his Dragunov rifle, the accurized version of the AK-47 with telescopic sight, tumbled earthward.

Human and his men then advanced to link up with Johan Blaauw and his men at the top half of the easternmost trenches. Blaauw's platoon then started drawing fire from behind them, an area already cleared. He asked Human to give him covering fire while he returned to retake the area. It was then that Human and Blaauw found that a feature, which they had been told by the photo-reconnaissance people was a track through the bush, was in fact a two-metre-deep and two-metre-wide trench running straight out of the base. It was packed with SWAPO soldiers using it as an escape route. Sergeant Peter Manderson was ordered to take some men and prevent any further escapes down this veritable highway to freedom. With a couple of LMGs, Manderson began firing on the fleeing escapees. The trench quickly turned into a death trap for the estimated 90 SWAPO soldiers caught inside as the machine-gunners had a duck shoot down the straight trench, the walls being too high to allow for easy exit.

Human's and Blaauw's platoons continued clearing the extensive trench system immediately in front of them, which were interspersed with large bunkers with thick pole-and-earth roofs, protecting them from mortar and bomb attacks. Each bunker was filled with around 20 SWAPO soldiers; the paratroopers found that the most effective way of clearing them was to drop a grenade down the ventilation funnels protruding from their roofs. The high explosive was devastating in the confined space with very few wounded making it to the surface to surrender.

Lieutenant Willie Jooste and his platoon, who had not seen much action by this time, found themselves in the extensive outdoor latrine area of the base. They had passed some trenches which bore the results of B Company's earlier ferocity; the few badly wounded SWAPO sheltering there were little threat. Jooste also came across a large bunker and, imitating Johan Blaauw, popped a grenade down the ventilation shaft. Like an earthquake, the roof of the bunker beneath his feet suddenly rose up as a store of explosives inside the bunker was detonated by the grenade. Jooste was shaken but unhurt, and took the precaution from then on to run like the wind after dropping a grenade down a vent.

Two paratroopers had been killed here and a handful wounded. Breytenbach himself had taken a bullet through the wrist which he bound up with a handkerchief to continue leading the assault. As mentioned, a warrant officer, Norman Reeves, was the recipient of the luckiest wound of the day. A bullet had hit him over the heart but had struck a pencil flare clipped in his pocket, bending it and forcing the bent part into his chest muscle. A shallow flesh wound resulted from something that on any other day would have killed him instantly.

The author approached the far trenches from behind because they were orientated to defend the base from the expected direction of attack, not from the riverside of the base. By this time, the attack companies were running toward the trenches as the author came to a trench where an enemy soldier, with his drum-fed PPSh sub-machine gun propped up on the pile of earth, was firing his weapon on full automatic. Leaning over the trench, the author could see that the enemy soldier had his eyes tightly shut. The author tapped him on the shoulder with his rifle barrel, in an attempt to get him to surrender. The soldier turned and opened his eyes to the sight of a paratrooper looming over him. He tried desperately to swing his still-chattering gun onto the new enemy but was promptly shot in the head.

Once the big guns were silenced the battle began to wind down. There were isolated skirmishes and firefights with pockets of stubborn SWAPO resistance as well as with a number of snipers, some using the Dragunov Soviet semi-automatic sniper rifles with telescopic sights. Such pockets were quickly mopped up and the paratroopers started thinking of home. The demolition teams were busy blowing up anything that could be used for war-making in the future and an intelligence team was scanning through the huge volumes of military documentation found in the headquarters building.

One of the paratroopers, Jan Volschenk, found a SWAPO soldier's notebook, which he only revealed just before publication of this book. In this notebook is the complete military hierarchy of the SWAPO command at Cassinga. This document finally puts paid to SWAPO's affirmation that Cassinga was a refugee camp.

CHAPTER SEVEN: CASSINGA BASE IS TAKEN

It was now past noon. The first wave of helicopters had been planned to extract half the attacking force at ten o'clock, two hours earlier. The delay in regrouping and forming up after the drop was now being felt at the tail end of the battle.

An improvised field hospital had been established next to the SWAPO hospital building where enemy and paratrooper wounded were treated by a paratrooper doctor and some medics. Any stray civilians, women and children were instructed to go there as it was the safest location on the base. At this stage it was now known that three paratroopers had been killed: Eddie Backhouse, Mark Kaplan and J.C. de Waal. Eleven paratroopers were wounded, two seriously, with another six hurt in one way or another on landing. It had not yet become apparent that Skillie Human was missing. He was last seen exiting the aircraft by the jumper behind him, who recollected that Human's parachute seemed to be descending much quicker than his. This is fairly common in mass jumps due to the weight difference between paratroopers, the loads they carry and the presence of small, localized thermals which can dramatically affect descent rates. Because of the sticks being split by the river, many paratroopers did not catch up to their designated fighting units until late in the battle, if at all. Skillie Human was therefore not missed until a roll call was done on reaching South West Africa where a consolidation was made between those who had left on the first wave of helicopters and those on the last.

SWAPO's losses on the other hand were massive. The bombing at the beginning of the attack, while not very effective because of the soft ground and indifferent aim—thanks to the huge amount of dust and debris thrown into the air by the first wave of bombs—did kill a number of SWAPO, but not nearly the amount hoped for, particularly on the parade ground where the daily muster parade was taking place. Many more were killed around the big anti-aircraft guns and in the trenches and a large number were killed by the stopper groups when they attempted to escape the box-drop around the base. The many snipers who were shot out of their trees added to the tally and, inevitably, a few people in civilian clothes also killed in the crossfire and by the bombing. It should be noted here that some people in civilian clothes, together with a following of small children, trailed A Company during the initial attack. They had to be regularly herded back so as not to get themselves shot by the defenders or to compromise the position of the attacking group. One of these children, a small boy, pleaded with Colonel Breytenbach to take him back to his parents in South West Africa. He was probably one of the abductees SWAPO kidnapped in order to disguise Cassinga as a refugee camp. It was heart-breaking for the paratroopers to have to leave these children behind because of the lack of helicopters to evacuate them.

While the paratroopers were cleaning up the pockets of resistance and the intelligence group was collecting documents from the headquarters buildings, Brigadier du Plessis suddenly became very animated. He had picked up on his purloined radio a message from the Skymaster DC-4 patrolling the border and eavesdropping on enemy radio communications, that the Cuban detachment at Techamutete was on its way to Cassinga to investigate the situation. It is unknown how the Cubans discovered that their SWAPO ally was being attacked but it was likely that the Cassinga SWAPO commander, Dimo Amaambo (spelt Amambo in the PLAN soldier's captured notebook) who had scurried away from the scene of the battle at its inception, had fled to friendly forces at Techamutete and raised the alarm. The South Africans were fairly confident that they had effectively jammed most of the radio communications which could have emanated from Cassinga before the bombers destroyed the radio aerials at the base. It was known that there was a flight of MiG fighters based at Techamutete as well as an armoured group of tanks and armoured personnel carriers with an infantry element. Du Plessis, on hearing that the Cubans were on their way, insisted that the helicopters be summoned immediately to start the evacuation of the paratroopers. Colonel Breytenbach vehemently disagreed, insisting that the helicopter LZs be secured before the helicopters were called. Once Breytenbach was happy that the

Charred SWAPO corpses outside a destroyed barrack block.

A casevac helicopter approaches a 'hot' LZ that is taking enemy fire.

PLAN officers' quarters with SWAPO dead in the foreground.

intelligence group was ready to leave with their voluminous piles of documents and a selection of prisoners to take back for questioning, he consented for the first lift of helicopters to come in. The planning called for 12 Puma helicopters for the first lift, eleven of which were to transport half the paratroopers to the HAA, refuel and wait for the call to uplift the remaining paratroopers at the base.

With the helicopters already on finals, the colonel asked one of his FACs, Frans Botes, to divert the helicopters from the bullet-swept LZs, Ramsey and Caroline, to the safer LZ Rennex to the east. He now had to make the best of a very undesirable situation. Because the designated helicopters could not land at their particular LZs, the well-organized numbering system was abandoned. Instead of Major Blikkies Blignaut, the other FAC, shepherding the troops to their correct helicopters in a planned and organized manner, an ad hoc allocation of available paratroopers was sent to the first available helicopter. This had the effect of leaving some behind who should have been on the first wave and taking some who should have been on the second. The commanding officer was left with a mishmash of approximately half his force to finish the battle and take on the approaching Cubans. To compound the mess made of the meticulous planning, Brigadier du Plessis was suddenly very much more noticeable. He was scurrying about, herding paratroopers onto helicopters so that the most rapid departure possible could be effected.

A Company should have left first, together with B Company, but they stayed behind. D Company, which was meant to protect the southern flank from interference by the Techamutete threat, left for the HAA with the first lift. Half the force was left to counter the armour and finish the battle.

In actual fact, Breytenbach called in only five of the helicopters as he was unsure of the complete safety of the LZ and run-in paths of the helicopters. One of these five was loaded with four bulging trunks of documentation taken from Amaambo's offices. Because of the disjointed nature of the para drop, many paratroopers who

A Puma casevac helicopter hovers above an LZ to uplift wounded paras.

Col Breytenbach (second from right) is debriefed by his commanders.

were meant to be extracted on the first lift were not yet at their designated LZs. It was planned that a select group of 16 prisoners would be lifted out with the first wave, this was altered at the last minute by the battalion second-in-command insisting that some of the more seriously wounded paratroopers be lifted out instead. This well-meaning change in plan actually endangered these wounded soldiers because, instead of waiting for the second lift, and then flying directly to either Ondangwa or Eenhana in South West Africa, they would be stranded at the HAA without any medical facilities while the helicopters refuelled before flying back to uplift the remaining troops. The helicopter crews at the HAA did their best to care for the wounded stranded there and when the second flight of six Pumas comprising the remainder of the first wave returned from Cassinga, they brought a doctor with them from the field hospital which had been established earlier at Cassinga. As it turned out, the premature evacuation of the critically wounded was fortuitous as they would have been a hindrance in the forthcoming battle with the Cuban armoured relief column which was about to come into play. Although the wounded stranded at the HAA would only be transported to South West Africa late in the afternoon, none succumbed to their wounds and all made full recoveries.

The two South African Engineer Corps officers who had jumped into Cassinga and were responsible for demolitions, also left with the first wave. This was before they had completed their task of demolishing all significant buildings and heavy weaponry. They left with all their fuses, charges and detonators, so no one else could complete the planned demolition job. It must be said however, that the ammunition stores around the base were doing a good job of demolishing the base on their own. These held large quantities of anti-tank mines and other explosives and were cooking off at irregular intervals, blowing the buildings and their contents to smithereens.

Arriving with the first wave of helicopters was a TV cameraman accompanied by a dapper, older soldier wearing a strange dark blue beret. Unheralded and unexpected, the Chief of the Army, Lieutenant General Constand Viljoen made an unobtrusive entry to the base. Colonel Breytenbach had enough to worry about without having to concern himself with the safety of another senior officer on his battlefield but he welcomed the general and quickly briefed him on the battle. The general made a quick tour of the base, noticing the large groups of prisoners sitting around the parade ground. Some of them were singing and clapping their hands, praising the *Boula* as they called the Boers. Some could speak Fanagalo, the pidgin *lingua franca* of the South African gold mines, and some had a smattering of Afrikaans, indicating that they had worked on the mines and perhaps for Afrikaans farmers in South West Africa at some stage. The prisoners were wearing a motley collection of uniforms. Most wore the Soviet chevron-patterned, ankle-high leather combat boot, whose tread pattern was so familiar to the paratroopers who had, as Fire Force troops, chased similarly shod SWAPO soldiers across countless miles of Owamboland's flat and featureless plains. The prisoners wore Cuban olive-drab pants and shirts with a mixture of belt types, one or two of which looked suspiciously like the South African-issue web belts. Headgear was a mixture of Cuban forage caps,

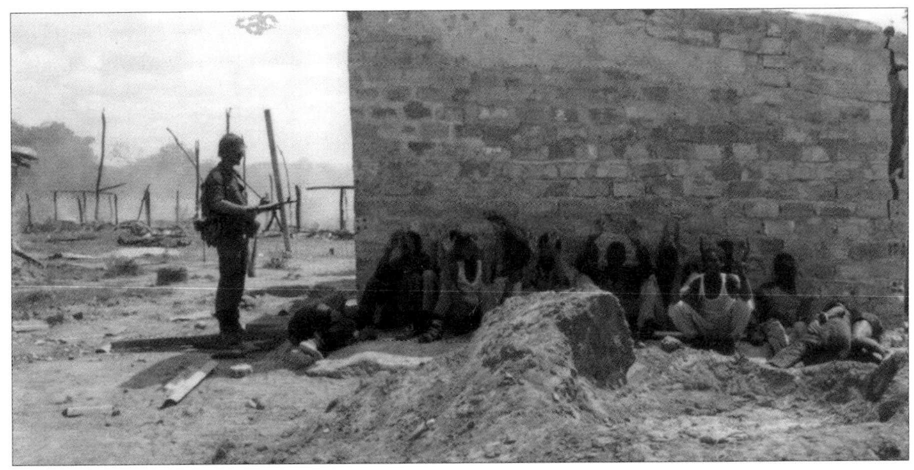

A para stands guard over POWs, most in civilian clothes. Three of them, lying on their sides, appear wounded. The ruins of Cassinga Base smoulder in the background.

woollen beanies and in one instance, a Russian fur cap with a USSR Communist Party red star badge.

The remaining paratroopers busied themselves with disabling all the vehicles and booby-trapping them and any remaining ammunition dumps they could find. They then formed up near the field hospital so as to proceed in an orderly manner to the LZs where they were to be picked up by the final wave of helicopters.

Prisoners under guard near the vehicle park. Most are women, with at least two children visible. Whether they are guerrilas, camp followers, refugees or abductees is almost impossible to ascertain. One woman in the centre of the group appears to have soiled herself, unsurprisingly.

A para offers a walking-wounded comrade a drink from his canteen. At left are SWAPO prisoners of war.

A mixed bag of male and female prisoners, with some of the men quite clearly wearing military uniforms.

With Cassinga still burning fiercely, paras regroup in preparation for evacuation. A captured recoilless rifle is in their midst.

CHAPTER EIGHT: CUBANS TO THE RESCUE

Prisoners on the parade ground. In the foreground enemy weapons and matériel are discarded on the parapet of a trench.

It was around one o' clock in the afternoon, three hours later than the planned extraction. A single Buccaneer circling the base had spotted an armoured column approaching Cassinga from Techamutete. The Cubans had finally roused themselves and were riding to the rescue. The column consisted of about 40 vehicles, 20 armoured personnel-carriers (APCs) of the Soviet BTR 152 type and as many as five T-34 Soviet tanks. Leading the column was a T-34 tank with its commander standing in the turret like "a curious meerkat" as one of the paratroopers later described it. Some thin-skinned trucks filled with troops and towing anti-aircraft cannon brought up the rear—all in all, about 300 Cuban and FAPLA soldiers. The column was promptly attacked by the lone Buccaneer with rockets and 30mm cannon, firing more than 50 rockets at the leading APCs, destroying three. The pilot then had to return to Grootfontein to re-arm. The remaining 170-odd paratroopers were now on their own, outnumbered by a factor of almost two to one and outgunned by a large margin. Apart from the paratroopers armed with rifles, light machine guns and grenades, the only heavier weaponry the South Africans could muster was an anti-tank platoon with ten two-man RPG teams, commanded by Lieutenant Pierre Hough and Staff Sergeant Derek Hopkins.

The foresight of the operation planners was now made evident when the T-34 tank leading the column detonated one of the large number 8 anti-tank mines that the Anti-Tank Platoon had laid earlier in the day for just such an eventuality. Nine mines had been laid across the approach road in a spread-out W formation. Great care had been taken to conceal the mines and all boot prints had been erased from the dusty road. The Anti-Tank Platoon had then withdrawn 300 metres to lie in ambush with their RPG rocket launchers. Someone with access to a radio then gave the Anti-Tank Platoon, which had by now been reinforced by Aulf Petterson and Gerald Harris, orders to withdraw further in the direction of Cassinga and re-lay their ambush there. This left the minefield killing ground uncovered by ambush and, should

A welcome sight for the paras: a South African Air Force aircraft attacks the Cuban/FAPLA armoured column.

"At 13h45 between 20 and 30 armoured cars were reported as being en route from the nearby Angolan military base at Techumutete, which also housed Cuban troops. Later, other troop carriers were spotted moving toward Kassinga. These convoys were attacked from the air and many were destroyed. According to information drawn from the Cuban archives, approximately 150 Cuban troops died in these attacks: the most serious casualty loss in their involvement in Angola."

—*The South African Truth and Reconciliation Commission Vol 2*, Chapter 2, 'The State Outside South Africa between 1960–1990'

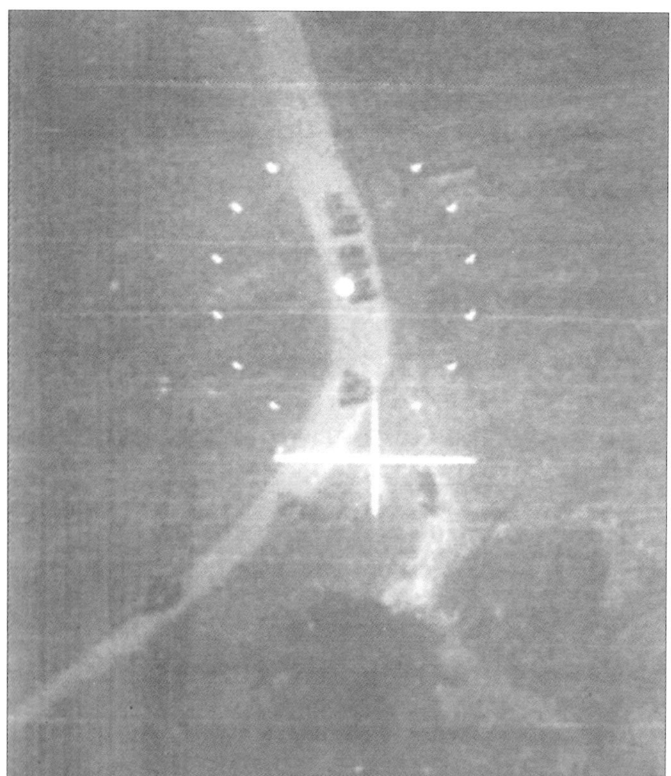

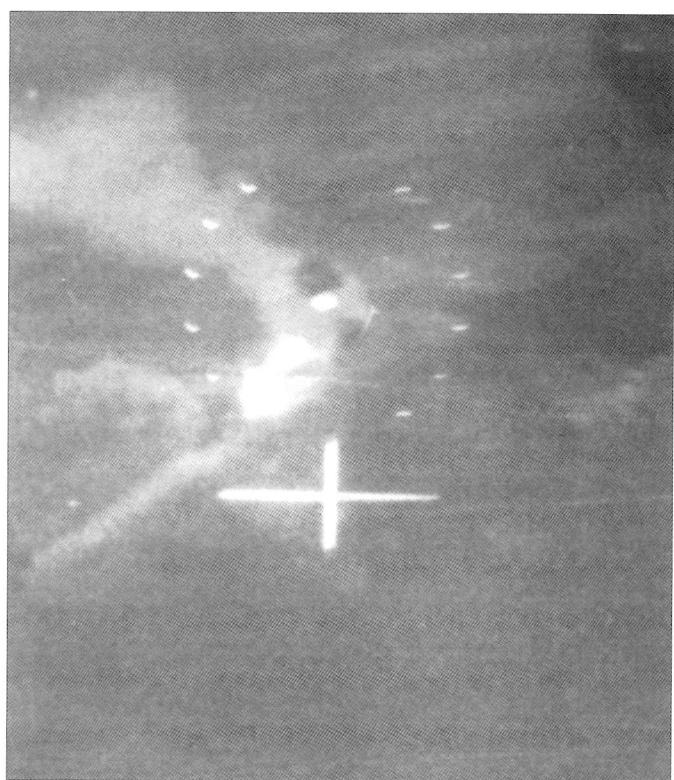

Gun camera photos of the Cuban/FAPLA armoured column taken from an attacking Mirage.

A mangled Cuban foot: the macabre evidence of a direct RPG-7 hit on a human body.

it eventuate, make halting an armoured column more difficult. The Anti-Tank Platoon was getting restless as the prospect of worthwhile action dissipated by the minute. They had until now only had to deal with the odd SWAPO soldier trying to escape the battlefield. This was not what they had hoped for. They had practised with the unfamiliar communist weapons during the training phase at De Brug and had become familiar with the peculiarities of the RPG. It had taken them some time to realize that an RPG is a counter-intuitive weapon, where the operator needs to aim off in a downwind direction when shooting in a crosswind. The reason for this is that the long tail of the rocket gets blown sideways by the crosswind, thus steering the rocket into the wind. So instead of behaving like any other weapon with the projectile being deflected downwind, the RPG is deflected upwind. This practice session was to prove its worth at Cassinga.

The noise of battle from the base behind the Anti-Tank Platoon had abated and was now confined to the ammunition in the magazines cooking off. Suddenly four or five BTR 152s burst out of the bush directly ahead of the platoon. These vehicles must have taken a short cut through the bush and avoided the minefield. The BTRs were driving in a loose V formation and were overflowing with Cuban soldiers and what J.C. van Wyk described as SWAPO but who were almost certainly FAPLA troops from Techamutete. The lead BTR was carrying about 40 soldiers, many of whom were draped over the armoured sides of the vehicle or standing up in the open-topped passenger compartment. They were singing and shouting and waving their rifles about in a noisy display of victory, presumably assuming that the attacking force had left the scene when the first wave of helicopters had flown off.

Derek Hopkins was the first paratrooper to react. He got to his feet and sent an RPG rocket into the rear of the lead BTR. The resultant explosion sent Cuban and FAPLA bodies flying into the air. Some who survived the first explosion stumbled out of the BTR and ran toward the shelter of a nearby building, led by a Cuban officer. Hopkins's second rocket took the officer squarely in the back just as he was entering the building, which served to demolish the building as well as the troops taking refuge inside.

Gerald Harris, assisted by Aulf Petterson, had also intended to take out the first BTR with his RPG, but had left the safety catch on the launcher in the 'on' position. By the time the empty click had registered the fact, Hopkins had already dealt with the threat. Harris then swung his RPG at the rapidly approaching second BTR and put a rocket into its left flank. Simultaneously, another rocket from someone on the other side of the ambush position penetrated the right-hand side of the BTR causing a combined explosion of spectacular dimensions. Cuban and FAPLA troops began streaming out of the stricken vehicle as Petterson took up

A lone Buccaneer wreacked havoc with the approaching Cuban armoured column. *Source: From Fledgling to Eagle*

A Mirage FIII AZ dropping cluster bombs. *Source: Vlamgat*

his R1 and at almost point-blank range began dropping the fleeing soldiers. Harris in the meantime was tracking and shooting his RPG at another BTR. Hearing a lull in the rifle fire from his number two, Harris glanced around and saw the cherry-red face of Petterson. He had been surprised by Harris's tracking movement of his RPG and had caught the edge of the RPG back-blast full in the face. Harris had the opportunity of having another shot at the fourth BTR which, seemingly oblivious to its companions' destruction, trundled on into the ambush. He hit it just above the front ridge but the BTR's momentum carried it into the killing ground, right into the arcs of fire of the paratroopers' LMGs and R1s. A dazed Cuban officer was seen wandering about some nearby buildings, waving his pistol in the air. Petterson finished him off with his R1. One of the armoured vehicles, probably a BRDM with a 14.5mm gun mounted in a turret came into view. The turret gun started firing at the paratroopers but before the gunner could cause any damage, two RPG rockets smashed into the base of the turret, severing it from the main body of the tank and at the same time bisecting the gunner. Those FAPLA and Cuban troops still alive hurriedly debussed directly into the killing ground, attempting to flee the withering rifle and LMG fire directed at them. Those who managed to escape the main ambush ran straight into the ambush stopper group and were picked off one by one. Breytenbach, hearing the heavy fighting, called Pierre Hough, the Anti-Tank Platoon commander, to hear how the defence was going. He then heard for the first time that the ambush had been moved right to the outskirts of the base and that he did not have the expected 500-metre buffer zone between the troops awaiting evacuation and the tanks. Furthermore, Hough informed him that they couldn't hold their position for much longer because the platoon was almost out of RPG rockets. The proximity of the defending paratroopers to Cassinga meant that the tanks would be able to get uncomfortably close to the two southern LZs, Senderling and Harris.

The Buccaneer that had been circling Cassinga had by now left Grootfontein, refuelled and re-armed, ready for the second phase of Operation *Reindeer*, the attack by Frank Bestbier and his men on the base Chetequera just north of the border. Colonel Breytenbach, now re-acquainted with his B25 radio and operator, was able to talk to Tac HQ and request immediate air support. He also learned through his FAC, Major Blikkies Blignaut, that the second wave of helicopters had been delayed by the unnecessary ferrying of wounded to the HAA area and that they were still in the process of fuelling up and would be some time in coming. Tac HQ agreed that the situation was unravelling and scrambled the Mirages at Ondangwa to help destroy the tanks. These aircraft, however, were not armed for anti-tank work, but with air-to-air missiles and 30mm HE cannon rounds for their anticipated task of preventing the MiG-19s and -21s based at Techamutete from attacking ground troops or helicopters.

Meanwhile Captain Dries Marais in his Buccaneer was on his way to Chetequera to help Frank Bestbier in his attack on the SWAPO base camp, Vietnam. Contrary to his orders and against the wishes of his armourer, Marais had, on a hunch, re-armed his aircraft with armour-piercing as well as high-explosive rockets. While in the air, he heard on the radio from Dick Warneke, the pilot of another Buccaneer returning for refuelling, that the paratroopers were in some difficulty with an armoured column. Marais decided off his own bat to abandon his mission to Chetequera and go to the aid of the paratroopers instead. He had heard the Mirages being scrambled but knew that his Buccaneer was better equipped to take on tanks. He also knew that the Mirages' fuel would only allow seven or eight minutes over target before they would have to head home to refuel. He hooked up with the two Mirages and charged to Cassinga to help the paratroopers catch their helicopter rides home.

The prospect of tanks sweeping through LZ Rennex, mowing down paratroopers and shooting down helicopters was a strong possibility. Breytenbach ordered Commandant Monty Brett to redeploy south and southwest of LZ Rennex which was situated between the base cemetery and Cassinga itself. The cemetery had been aptly designated in planning as the emergency RV for all the paratroopers in the event of the evacuation going awry. The colonel now decided to implement the emergency withdrawal plan and break contact with FAPLA and the Cubans and start moving toward the distant HAA. He asked the helicopters to

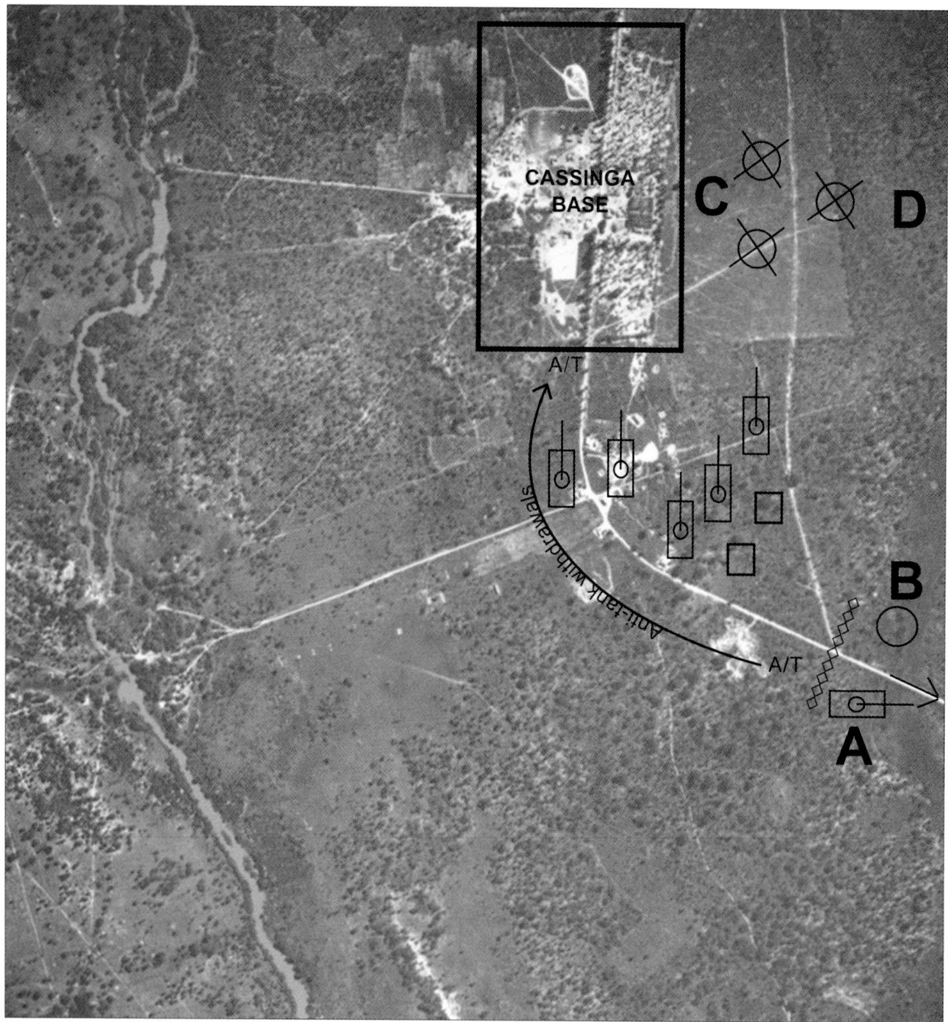

→ to Techamutete
minefield
tank positions
A/T Anti-tank ambush positions
BTRs
helicopters

A: first tank destroyed in the minefield
B: AA Gun
C: LZ Rennex
D: east to Eenhana

It is important to note that the SWAPO defensive trench systems were highly developed on the eastern side of the base, adjacent to and facing LZ Rennex.

take off immediately, refuelled or not. They could pick up the paratroopers along the way to the HAA where they could refuel if necessary. The paratroopers were ordered to move to the LZ and form a protective circle so as to have a mobile airhead where the helicopters could safely land.

The Anti-Tank Platoon was now withdrawing to LZ Rennex so as to immediately board their helicopters once they eventually arrived. The platoon was taking fire from the roof of a building between them and the LZ. The race for the LZ was on. Some Cuban and FAPLA troops had outflanked them, preventing them from reaching the rest of the force awaiting extraction. The platoon engaged the Cubans in a fierce firefight but because the paratroopers were out in the open, they were unable to attack the building effectively. One of the paratroopers, losing patience with the enemy, stood up with his RPG and while shouting an obscenity at them, sent a rocket into the roof, blowing six enemy troops off the roof and into the platoon's line of fire.

The two Mirages then arrived on the scene, closely followed by Dries Marais's Buccaneer. This small aerial armada was cheered by the paratroopers as it pounced onto the armoured column, the Mirages firing their cannons at the thin-skinned BTRs and the Buccaneer releasing its rockets at the more formidably protected tanks. This assault immobilized most of the remaining vehicles in the column with the surviving troops scattering into the surrounding bush. Lieutenant Dolf du Plessis described the aerial attack as a spinning coin moving in three dimensions: the aircraft diving steeply onto the column, firing their ordnance, then pulling steeply upward and looping over the top to come back again, at the same angle but in a different direction. This choreography served to confuse the enemy anti-aircraft gunners who had unlimbered their guns from the trucks and were attempting to drive the aircraft off.

The Mirages, having reached 'Bingo' status (enough fuel to reach base), had to return to Ondangwa after less than ten minutes over the target, but the longer range of the Buccaneer enabled it to stay on station for much longer.

Marais was hoarding his rockets, knowing that he was the last line of defence for the inadequately armed paratroopers awaiting extraction. On completing a circuit of the base, he asked his navigator to arm the remaining 12 rockets so as to enable him to eliminate the armour still on the road to Cassinga. During his low-level approach, he was greeted by heavy fire from small arms and anti-aircraft guns. Lining up his sights on the remainder of the convoy, he pressed the firing button, only to hear and see nothing. The 12 rockets he thought he had in reserve had been fired sometime during the mad mêlée of his first runs at the column. The Buccaneer was out of ammunition just when it was most needed. The remaining tanks were firing on the paratroopers in their positions of all-round defence in their LZ. The helicopters were coming in and were at their most vulnerable—during landings and take-offs—especially when overloaded and in the hot, high-altitude conditions of Cassinga.

One particular tank was threatening disaster. It had charged ahead toward the paratroopers and was firing its cannon and machine guns as it went. Marais executed another circuit, this time tight and steep, and although under increasingly effective fire from the anti-aircraft guns of the column, took his aircraft down to below treetop level and approached the offending tank by flying up the road at zero altitude. The paratroopers saw the almost silent, ghostlike apparition hissing up the road toward them at lorry height. As it passed, the hiss turned into the deafening roar of two Rolls-Royce Spey jet engines at full thrust. This transition from silence to bedlam was caused by a shockwave being pushed ahead of the Buccaneer as it approached Mach 1 and it turned out to be almost as effective as the recently exhausted armour-piercing rockets. The offending tank was rocked and buffeted by the blast with the paint seared from the tank's skin by the full blast of the jet's hot gasses as it passed mere feet from the turret.

The tank stopped in its tracks and while Marais was pulling many Gs in another tight circuit, it reversed and took refuge behind a small hillock which prevented it from firing directly at the paratroopers. While this unconventional aerial assault was in progress, the helicopters were arriving to pick up the last of the paratroopers.

The planned LZs were all either under fire from the Cuban and FAPLA forces or were too far away from the main body of paratroopers who had gathered at the emergency assembly point at the cemetery. The concept of the mobile LZ was working well in that helicopters were being protected while landing but that protection was being depleted with every load of paratroopers extracted.

The Anti-Tank Platoon was conducting a spirited defence, running backward to its LZ while firing at targets of opportunity. Because the LZ was not cleared or prepared in any way, the helicopter pilots were obliged to choose their own landing areas between the tall trees and low bushes studding the area. This meant that the usual helicopter emplaning drills were dispensed with as no orderly line could form because no one knew where the helicopters would land.

This also meant that the alphabetical allocation system was unworkable. Paratroopers quickly gave up trying to find their allocated aircraft and merely hopped aboard the nearest convenient helicopter. The flight engineers became temporary bus conductors, ejecting indignant paratroopers from overloaded helicopters. One such ejected trooper was heard to shout above the whining turbines of a Super Frelon, "But sarge, I've got a season ticket!"

The LZ was still under intense fire from tanks and depressed anti-aircraft guns but luckily, because of Marais in his Buccaneer, the fire was inaccurate and ineffective. Marais had not stopped buzzing the armoured column and was picking up some very accurate fire for his pains. A 14.5 shell hit his armoured windshield dead centre but failed to penetrate and his engines took two AA rounds but didn't even hiccup. His wings and tail were riddled with small-arms strikes but he soldiered on as the sole threat to the opposition while the paratroopers emplaned.

CHAPTER NINE: GOING HOME

The apparent chaos of the emergency extraction on the mobile LZ was sorting itself out as more and more paratroopers found their way onto empty helicopters. Some prisoners who had been commandeered into bearing stretchers carrying the dead and badly wounded were also trying to board the helicopters, which probably meant they were unwilling soldiers, press-ganged by SWAPO. They were naturally summarily ejected to make room for the intended passengers. The author was passed by an older, grey-haired soldier bearing no rank badges and beaten to a Puma by a good few lengths. This rankless dust-cloud turned out to be General Constand Viljoen who had flown in with the first wave of helicopters to personally observe the battleground. Like the rest of the attackers, he had been taken by surprise by the Cuban and FAPLA armoured column. Fearing capture, the general had hidden his epaulette badges under a stone and thus appeared to be just another rifleman, albeit older that the rest. The author was asked to get off the helicopter as it was overloaded, so he dismounted grumpily to await another lift home. The Puma lumbered into the air, nose down to try and pick up some airspeed before having to hop over some high trees in front of it. Running out of room, the pilot zigged-zagged to maximize space, as the bottom of the fuselage scraped the tops of the trees.

Another Super Frelon descended into the dust cloud stirred up by the previous helicopter and its departing general and the author gratefully hopped aboard. As the body of Eddie Backhouse was loaded into the Super Frelon, a large explosion just to the rear of the helicopter rocked it violently forward on its wheels. The tanks were finding their range and things were getting hot. The author broke out the last of his beers and handed them round to his fellow passengers, getting a dirty look from another high-ranking officer already seated in the Frelon. When cigarettes followed, the officer appeared set to erupt but said nothing, perhaps because his rank badges were also sitting under a rock near the cemetery. The celebrations continued for the entire flight despite the constant threat of MiGs being scrambled from Techamutete to attack the helicopters.

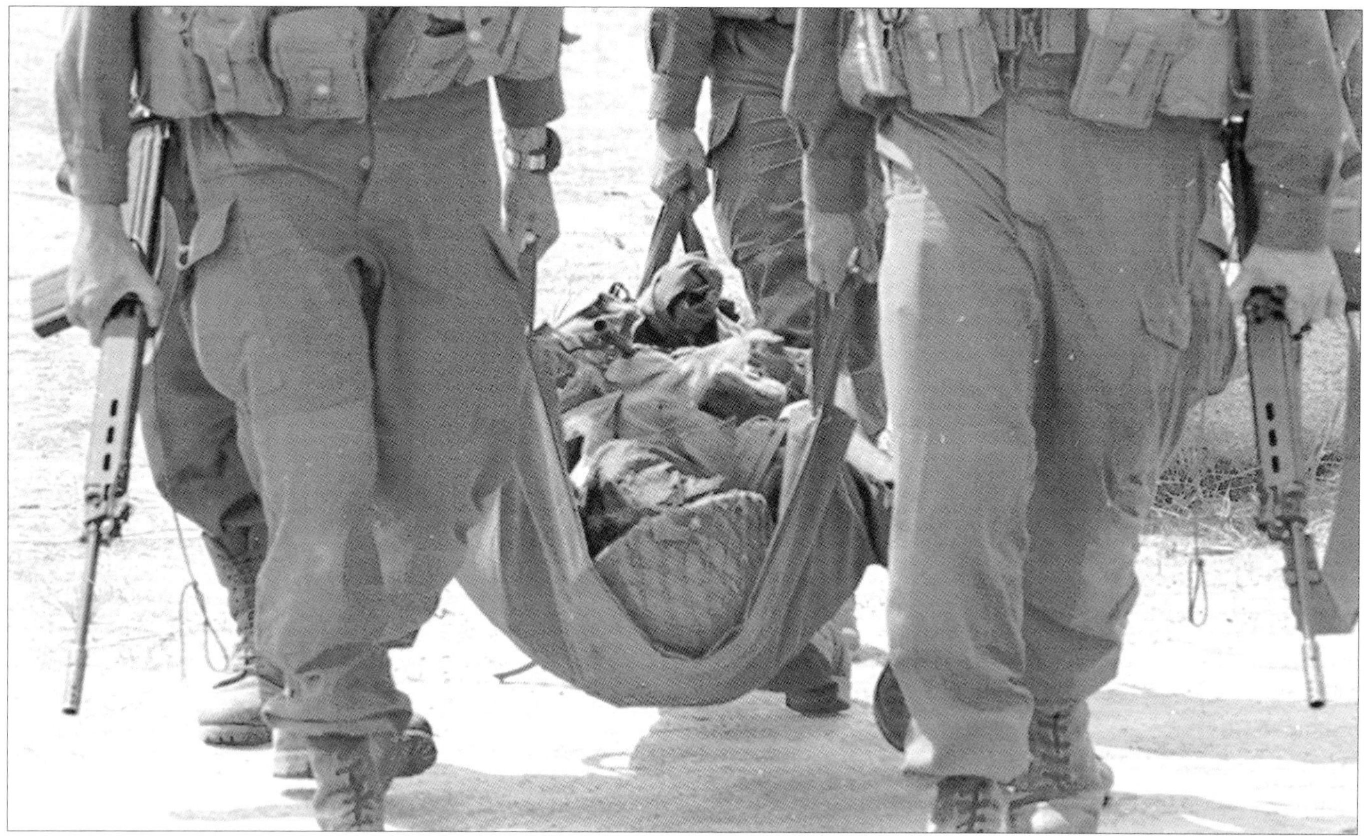

The body of a para is carried to an LZ for uplift back to South West Africa.

Puma pilot John Church taking a last flight around Cassinga before final evacuation, searching for any stray paras. Quite fortuitously he spotted Sergeant Peter Manderson alone on the ground and picked him up. Manderson had become separated from his unit and, without any form of communication, would have undoubtedly been left behind had it not been for the diligent pilot.

Weary but satisfied paras stop over at Ondangwa on their way home.

Meanwhile, John Church, the pilot of the last helicopter to land, was lifting off under heavy fire. Because Church knew that the loading system had been compromised and that there was no indication that all the paratroopers had actually made it to the mobile LZ, he decided to make a circuit of Cassinga to ensure no one had been left behind. This saved Sergeant Peter Manderson a long walk home or worse. Manderson had become separated from his company and was wandering about with no communications with anyone, when he saw the last wave of helicopters lifting off a few hundred metres away. As Church made his circuit under fire, he spotted Manderson, swooped in and hovered while a greatly relieved Manderson was hauled aboard by willing hands.

The last helicopter out of Cassinga then made haste to catch up with the gaggle heading at low level toward the border. Due to low fuel levels, the last wave was put down at Eenhana, an SADF base just south of the border. Dusk was falling on the helicopters as they landed on the long dirt strip. The tired but happy paratroopers found tents and mattresses and prepared to get some much-needed sleep. Many had not slept for 36 hours since waking the day before in Bloemfontein.

A final roll call was taken and compared with the roll call from Ondangwa where the casualties and the troops from the first wave were staying. After much deliberation between company and platoon commanders it seemed that everyone was accounted for, apart from Skillie Human. The paratroopers had suffered three killed in action: Backhouse, Kaplan and de Waal, 12 wounded and one missing in action. Despite the lateness of the hour and the exhaustion there was a flood of volunteers who wanted to go back and try to find Human. A delegation was sent to the command structure to organize a helicopter and failing that, a fixed-wing aircraft to allow the men to jump into Cassinga again. The plan was rejected due to the high vigilance of the Angolan defences after the two raids into their territory.

The infantry unit at Eenhana pulled out all the stops for the paratroopers and provided a good hot meal of steak and mielie meal along with their entire stock of beer. After the meal, the paratroopers spread themselves about the base, some in tents and some on the sand revetments around the airstrip to sleep the sleep of the just.

Early the next morning, the helicopters, having been refuelled during the night, lifted the men out to Ondangwa, the main air base in Owamboland. At Ondangwa the paratroopers were ordered to form up on the apron before boarding the C-130s and C-160s to fly home to Bloemfontein.

Instead of the congratulatory speech expected, they were lectured on the inadvisability of trying to take any booty home with them. Each trooper's 'great bag' was searched for anything that had been picked up at Cassinga. The author had two 35mm still cameras and the now dysfunctional 16mm movie camera. When Commandant Archie Moore came to him, he asked what the hell he was doing with cameras. The commandant was told

After the battle, the author poses prior to evacuation.

that they were army cameras, apart from the Olympus OM1 which was private. The commandant then launched into a lecture on how illegal it was to have a private camera and demanded all the film from all the cameras. The author handed over all the exposed army film for both the 35mm and movie cameras and when the commandant demanded the film for the private camera, the author reluctantly reached into his pocket and handed over another three film canisters of film, which were of course unexposed films that had not been used. The private films which had been exposed were secreted in the bloused bottom of his pants legs. These films comprise all the colour photographs featured in this book. In addition, a pair of Soviet binoculars, a cheap Timex watch and a Russian fur hat with the Communist Party badge liberated from a Russian-looking soldier he had shot during the battle survived the search. The watch was given to the author's section leader Pat O'Leary who had lost his before the battle in Bloemfontein and had asked anyone coming across one to save it for him.

The paratroopers then boarded the big aircraft to take them back to Bloemfontein, before heading off to their individual residences. Some took trains, some buses and some were picked up by wives or parents if they lived nearby. The homecomings were subdued as security had been so tight that relatives back home were unaware that their loved ones had spent a few days out of the country. Only when the press releases emerged was it revealed that the Battle of Cassinga had been successfully executed.

CHAPTER TEN: A POTEMKIN REFUGEE CAMP: DEBUNKING SWAPO CLAIMS

The title of this chapter is taken from Grigori Aleksandrovich Potemkin (1739–1791) who reputedly ordered villages consisting of mere façades to be built along the route of a tour by Catherine the Great in order that she would think her peasants were leading happy and healthy lives.

For more than 30 years, the world has been puzzled about a few inexplicable anomalies in SWAPO's version of the battle. Firstly, why, when some of their soldiers fought so bravely at Cassinga, did SWAPO consistently maintain Cassinga was a refugee camp? Secondly, why would SWAPO kidnap a group of very young children from South West Africa and transport them 250 kilometres into Angola? They would be of no use to a guerrilla army for several years. Why not kidnap youngsters of a fighting age instead? Thirdly, if Cassinga was indeed PLAN's military headquarters, why has SWAPO steadfastly maintained the deception that it was only a refugee transit camp and the only casualties women and children?

To find the answer as to why SWAPO never recognized the extreme bravery of some of the defenders at Cassinga, we need to go back some years to the birth of the Shipanga faction. As mentioned earlier, Andreas Shipanga was a SWAPO founder at odds with Sam Nujoma in how the war was to be waged. Shipanga disagreed with Nujoma's strategy of getting involved in the Angolan fracas on the side of UNITA, South Africa's ally in the battle against the MPLA. He wanted instead to concentrate all efforts on defeating South Africa in South West Africa. Shipanga also accused Nujoma and his cohorts of rampant corruption. This difference in opinion led to Shipanga being arrested, along with hundreds of his supporters and sent to detention camps in Zambia and Tanzania. Shipanga himself was imprisoned with the rest of his men in the Mboroma Detention Camp at Kabwe, just north of Lusaka. After international demands for his release became too strident, he was later moved to Tanzania, where *habeas corpus* does not exist. The 1,000 Shipanga-faction prisoners were later joined by about 600 newly trained SWAPO soldiers from the USSR because they were suspected of being Shipanga sympathizers. These prisoners were systematically starved and some were shot by their Zambian guards. Shortly before the South African assault on Cassinga, they were transferred there. SWAPO had learned of the imminent attack from the highly placed Soviet spy, Dieter Gerhardt, based at the SADF communications centre, Silvermine, in the Cape Province. Nujoma saw that by placing his most belligerent fighters, albeit his most troublesome, in Cassinga, he would kill two birds with a single stone. The Shipanga soldiers were likely to be ferocious in battle against the hated Boers and were even more likely to be wiped out by the South Africans. Thus in one fell swoop he would permanently remove the Shipanga rebels from the SWAPO landscape while at the same time giving the Boers a bloody nose.

It was of course impossible for Nujoma to later acknowledge that the troublesome Shipanga faction could have fought so bravely at Cassinga. So, in order to keep their valiant actions under wraps, the pretence of Cassinga being a refugee camp only, was enthusiastically maintained.

The following letter appeared in *The Namibian* some years after SWAPO won the elections and took over the country:

> **Outraged by Attacks**
> I am extremely outraged by the verbal raids on our own party, SWAPO, against an infant party which has enriched our political spectrum with the system of addressing issues rather than individuals. The CoD [Congress of Democrats, a Namibian opposition party] has, to my knowledge, not targeted any particular party as an enemy. This, in normal politics, does not deserve an onslaught by the ruling party, its government and its President.
>
> There are two categories of party and government: those who have been at the top of the party from its inception and who know the whole truth about the party and the reality of the CoD on the one hand, and those leaders who did not have a chance to know their party because they did not leave the country to fight for independence. The latter group is best represented by comrade Jerry Ekandjo, who in his Cassinga Day speech at Elim, orchestrated his total ignorance of his party's own history. Almost everything he attributed to the new party actually fits his own, and I will prove it.
>
> Ekandjo believes the new party is a group of spies and traitors. Those who have listened (on radio) to Jerry's account of his struggle against apartheid have noticed that the Minister always mentioned all or some of the following as his colleagues and leaders in the struggle: Keshi Nathaniel Maxuilili, Frans Nangutuwala, Aaron Mushimba, Johannes Nangutuwala, Andreas Nuukwao, etc. They all went into exile. Keshi and Andreas were arrested by SWAPO but survived and are still alive outside the party. Aaron Mushimba spent years in the dungeons of Lubango (his sister, our current First Lady, followed him there). J. Nangutuwala was arrested and taken together with a kidnapped Louis Nelengani, former vice president of SWAPO and chief architect of PLAN, and both died in Angola in 1975. And his brother Frans, probably Ekandjo's closest comrade? He was arrested in

1976 at SWAPO's central base in western Zambia. He escaped, but was later killed.

Other SWAPO cadres and commanders such as Jackson Hamupembe, Theodor Shongoa, Gottlieb Nakaambo and Philipus Kalimba were, in 1977, asked to decide the positions they 'wanted' to be shot in while in pre-dug graves. All these were, by SWAPO's definition, 'traitors and spies' and had Jerry joined them in exile, he would have most likely been treated no differently.

Jerry also alleged that the CoD wanted to bring in white people, including the English and the Americans. But the truth is that they are already here, and not brought in by Ulenga. Who doesn't know that it is the two top leaders of our government who received honorary degrees from the same whites? We also know one of our top leaders is an honorary citizen of an American city, Atlanta. Is it not also true that one SWAPO and government leader owns a mansion in another American city, Philadelphia? What about bank accounts abroad? We all know when our government talks of 'friendly people' they mean the Americans, Germans and British. They make extensive trips to these countries and invite them to come and invest here.

"We have fought for this country, lost our lives and blood in Cassinga, Oshatotwa ..." lamented the Minister. But he doesn't know the truth about the Cassinga and Oshatotwa raids. The raid on Oshatotwa training camp in July 1976 has a history. The way the war was being administered led PLAN fighters to suspect the presence of SA agents in top leadership and consequently the military wing. For example, at the start of 1976, SWAPO's defence secretary, Peter Nanyemba, the chief suspect, ordered PLAN fighters to leave the 'major' island base in Kwando river for a 'minor' island that morning. They agreed but did not move. At about 16h00 that same day, the 'minor' island was under SA rocket and artillery fire. No one was hurt but the island was left in a dilapidated state by the 148 shells that fell on it. Just before that, the same defence secretary had ordered commander Peter Hambiya to have all the tents in Munyengani camp moved inwards and concentrated at the centre of the camp. (Hambiya himself stopped spending nights there.) The message of warning and advice from the island comrades made the guerrillas, under the commander of comrades, Nghidimondjila Shoombe and Festus Ashikoto, leave the camp that night (i.e. a day after the island bombing) for the central base. Sam Nujoma, Moses Garoeb and Mishake Muyongo, now and then ordered PLAN fighters to stop accusing the leadership of having spies among themselves and finally ordered the disarming and mass arrest (by the Zambian army) of the fighting force. But a few months later the same Nanyemba visited the remaining base—Oshatotwa training centre—and ordered the trainees to remain in camp. He left the camp and around 04h00 the next morning the camp was under South African mortar and helicopter attack. But all Nanyemba's commanders did not spend the night in that camp.

The arrested fighters (smeared by SWAPO as the Shipanga group)—about 2500 of them—became the Mboroma group who, according to Zambian captains, were supposed to be reduced by three-quarters through starvation and shooting. Starvation took its toll but the shootings of 5 August 1976 killed only three but wounded many. After the Zambian authorities refused to resume the shootings (the soldiers believed guerrillas were using witchcraft to evade the bullets!), most of the survivors, including Dr Vaino Shivute, were bundled off to Angola and dropped in Cassinga where the same Nanyemba gave them strange uniforms that looked more like those of Koevoet, and instructed them in case of an attack, to hide in a dungeon under a large thatched barrack. When the attack came, a PLAN defence unit that arrived later began shooting at these people too, probably thinking they were Koevoet.

It is alright for a Minister to campaign for his party, but it is wrong for him to accuse others of what his party is guilty of. Jerry is discrediting and probably politically destroying himself. It is high time he started talking to his surviving comrades such as Keshii and Nuukwao instead of totally depending on the views of others.

Ex-Combatant
Ondangua

Note: This letter has been shortened. The real name and address of the writer has been provided, and he informs *The Namibian* he was part of some of the historic occurrences he refers to above, and it is perhaps time to lift the unstated 'taboo' on discussion of controversial aspects of Namibia's past.

—Ed, Namibia, 1999

To find the answer to the assiduous and adamant claims that Cassinga was only a refugee camp, we need to go back to some time before the battle and into the funding and support that SWAPO enjoyed from the United Nations.

Ever since Resolution 435 was tabled and eventually passed in September 1978 by the United Nations, that august body looked favourably upon any pleas for help from SWAPO. Because its charter precluded it from giving military aid to revolutionary movements, the organization could only supply aid in the form of money, food and medicines, to children and refugees, usually through the offices of UNICEF and the UNHCR. SWAPO, with help from sophisticated Soviet advisers, was quick to seize the opportunity and obtain for itself—under the guise of having to support refugees—money, food and medicines intended for genuine humanitarian needs.

UNICEF was happy to supply SWAPO, so long as a modicum of respectability could be attached to these military camps. The UN had procedures and regulations which had to be fulfilled before the money could flow, and one of these was that 'refugee camps' had to be visited and 'certified'. Just such a 'certification' visit was scheduled by UNICEF to take place at Cassinga in April 1978. This of course presented SWAPO and PLAN with an immediate problem: how to disguise a military camp as a refugee camp. Naturally, all the weapons could be hidden in the bush but what of the trenches and bunkers? More critically, where were the masses of children and aged that any refugee camp should have? The trenches and bunkers which ringed the camp could possibly be explained away by saying that an attack was feared and these were shelters. The UN was known to turn a blind eye when these things were brought to their notice, but where to get the children that UNICEF was most concerned with helping? A simple but cleverly ruthless plan was devised on the lines of: If we don't have any of our own, we will steal some.

And this is how the great St Mary's abduction happened. On 21 February 1978, shortly before the scheduled arrival of the UNICEF inspection team at Cassinga, SWAPO abducted a group of 119 children and a teacher on its way to the mission school of St Mary's just over the border in Namibia. PLAN soldiers hijacked the group and walked them at gunpoint straight to Cassinga, 250 kilometres north of the border, and *voila!* ... dozens of kidnapped children aged from five to 15 were instantly turned into refugees and given a hastily cobbled-together classroom so that the UNICEF inspectors would have someone to whom they could open the sluice gates of aid.[1]

A similar abduction to harvest refugees occurred on the road between Ruacana and Oshakati on 22 April 1978, a few days before the attack on Cassinga, when a bus of 70 civilians, women and children, was hijacked and driven to Cassinga. These civilians arrived just in time for the UNICEF visit to the camp.[2]

The hijacked bus was found by the South African paratroopers when they attacked Cassinga.

Clearly, the UNICEF team were not totally stupid and in the Truth and Reconciliation Commission Report, it was said: "The fact that Kassinga had a non-military dimension is reflected in the UNICEF report of a visit by a UNICEF delegation from its regional office in Brazzaville, published two days before the raid." This wording is telling in that UNICEF does *not* say there was a "military dimension to the camp", the clear meaning being that Cassinga, the camp, was a military camp with some civilian elements.

That these refugee elements were entirely fabricated and artificial escaped the UNICEF inspectors entirely. The leader of the team who showed the UNICEF inspectors around the camp was none other than Dimo Amaambo, the supreme commander of PLAN in Angola, the same Dimo Amaambo who lived at Cassinga and miraculously escaped the attack on his home base by the South African paratroopers a few weeks later, thanks to Gerhardt. It took no great propaganda expert to quickly cook up the story that Cassinga was a refugee camp, because SWAPO had been fraudulently selling it as such to the UN for some time.

> Some 1,200 people—South West African, Angolan, Cuban and South African—died; over 600 others, overwhelmingly South West African and Angolan, were wounded in the attacks on Kassinga and Chetequera that day. It is probable that some died later from their wounds. In addition, several hundred were captured at Chetequera. No prisoners, or perhaps at most a handful, were taken from Kassinga. Those reported in the early despatches as being held as prisoners were released when no room on the evacuation helicopters was available for them.
>
> —*The South African Truth and Reconciliation Commission Volume 2*, Chapter 2, 'The State Outside South Africa between 1960 and 1990'

This meant that, after the battle, SWAPO was obliged to keep up the pretence that Cassinga was a refugee camp. Had they admitted that it was SWAPO's main military base, they would have been exposed as having deceived UNICEF and the UNHCR so as to fraudulently obtain money, food and sanitation equipment from this charitable yet naïve organization. The 'Potemkin' refugee camp was a propaganda success. UN aid has never stopped flowing to SWAPO in the 30 years since the original grand deception.

Steve Mvula, a Namibian Human Rights activist wrote about Cassinga in May 2010: "The SADF hated the truth [...] mostly when we need it the most. It is unfortunate that SWAPO has chosen, out of its own free will, to follow suit, hide the truth and propagate lies [...] sometimes. And representatives of the international press who visited Cassinga days after the attack were only allowed to see what was of propaganda value for SWAPO, and they apparently did not ask critical questions."

Mvula is bemoaning SWAPO's duplicity in depicting Cassinga as a refugee camp, housing only women and children. He goes on to challenge the official SWAPO version by examining each contradiction in their story: "But Cassinga was also a military base

---

1 "I received information from one former pupil who later stated that he had been abducted from St Mary's mission with the others. He was at Cassinga when the Boers suddenly arrived by parachute and he fled into the bush, running through a line of paratroopers who showed no interest in him or his fellow students but who kept moving forward into the battle that was beginning to pick up steam. Later on he was inducted into SWAPO and, finally, was captured by the Recces in Owamboland. He joined 5 Recce as an operator and was discharged after 1994. He subsequently ended up as a mercenary serving in various places in Africa."
—Colonel Jan Breytenbach in an email to the author, 9 September 2010.

2 "The shot-out bus we encountered at Cassinga was definitely the bus in which commuters from Ruacana to Oshakati were transported before they too were abducted by force. Of course, there could have been children among them as well. This latter abduction happened about three weeks before our attack on Cassinga and is also recorded as such [in the Occurrence Diary kept by Sector 10].
—Colonel Jan Breytenbach in an email to the author, 9 September 2010.

Captured communist weapons: used to defend innocent refugees?

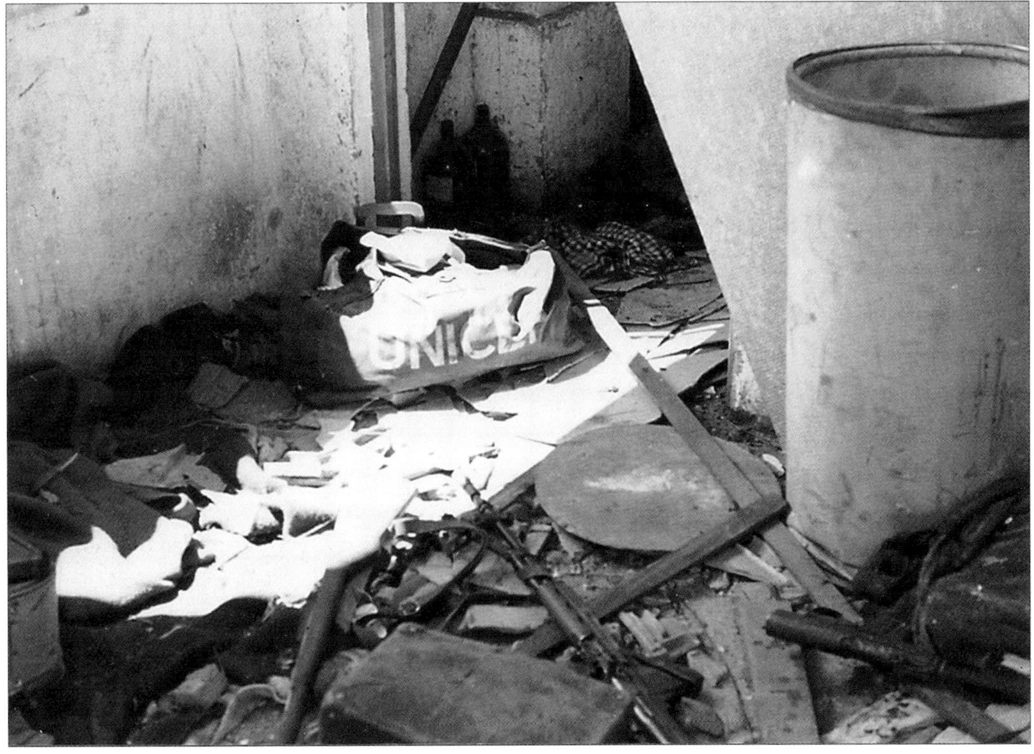

A UNICEF tog bag among the detritus of war, which includes a communist assault rifle.

in the sense that there were, according to SWAPO, 300 armed guerrillas in that 'refugee' camp. Senior People's Liberation Army of Namibia (PLAN) commander Jonas Haiduwa reportedly died in the Cassinga attack. Supreme PLAN Commander Dimo Hamaambo's [Amaambo's] house was also destroyed during the Cassinga attack. Now here come tough questions: what was guerrilla commander Haiduwa doing in or near a refugee camp? How was it possible that PLAN Commander Hamaambo had a house in a refugee camp?"

He accuses SWAPO and PLAN of internationally sanctioned illegal behaviour if their version is true: "A UN delegation that visited Cassinga days before the attack was guided through the camp by PLAN Commander Hamaambo [Amaambo] and PLAN Political Commissar Greenwell Matongo. Well, if Cassinga was a refugee camp, then it was abused by SWAPO to shelter its senior guerrilla commanders. If this was the case then the camp was clearly used as a human shield. Hence, SWAPO must bear the blame for placing hundreds of guerrilla fighters in a 'refugee camp', something strictly prohibited under international humanitarian law!"

Mvula asks why SWAPO insists that only women and children were killed at Cassinga when it was common knowledge, and practice, for a very large proportion of refugees fleeing South West Africa to be young men, men of military-service age. He states: "However, figures show that the majority of those who had died in the attack were men: 326 men and 256 women. Sometimes, Namibian women were also fighters and as such they were not always 'defenceless' civilians. And even if they were unarmed civilians, they were not defenceless. There was an armed contingent of 300 guerrillas whose task was to defend the camp and they apparently failed to defend [it]. They deserve the blame or at least their Commander-in-Chief who had failed to make sure they were appropriately armed."

Mvula then destroys SWAPO's boast that they had shot down three SADF aircraft and killed 102 SADF soldiers: "'Miracles at Cassinga' should have been the headline in all newspapers. Firstly, then SWAPO Information Secretary Peter Katjavivi told the world there was no single guerrilla fighter at Cassinga (who killed the 102 SADF soldiers then?). Secondly, PLAN Defence Secretary Peter Nanyemba confidently described how three SAAF aircraft were shot down over Cassinga during the attack. By whom and with what?"

He takes Sam Nujoma to task for falsely inflating the number of attacking SADF paratroopers so as to depict the battle as one-sided: "Thirdly, the biggest miracle was when SWAPO President Sam Nujoma told the world that four C-130 transport airplanes dropped 1,500 paratroopers at Cassinga (in other words, each C-130 plane miraculously transported 375 heavily armed troops). That is to be expected only from someone who is militarily illiterate."

Furthermore, he takes SWAPO to task when they finally admit that there was a small contingent of "lightly armed" guards at the camp: "Fourthly, the 'lightly armed' guerrillas that had killed 102 'Boers' and yet they had suffered no single casualty, was another miracle. But then later SWAPO also admitted there were at least two anti-aircraft gun emplacements at Cassinga. So, the 300 guerrillas were heavily armed after all because only a militarily illiterate person would say that, for example, a multi-barrelled Zenith 23mm anti-aircraft cannon is a light weapon!"

Mvula then dismisses the vacuous SWAPO claim that gas was used in the attack by the SADF: "That was simply not true. Those who were 'paralyzed' did so apparently because of self-induced fear after seeing the smoke from the burning huts (the same happened with those who claim to have sighted ghosts: they were paralyzed by fear and could not run for safety). Moreover, nobody has come forward, so far, to claim that he or she had seen the SADF attackers wearing gas masks because nerve gas does not discriminate. Wanted very urgently: the whole truth about Cassinga!" He ends off his penetrating critique by quoting other academics who have written on the reliability of SWAPO spokespersons: "Therefore, the history of what really happened in that memorable year of 1978 has yet to be written in full. As one political analyst of repute put it: 'Namibian leaders lie confidentially.' So far only the powerful, and their clients, have written about it, and their accounts manipulate and deform the facts and are filled with outright lies."

In another noteworthy article, published in the Namibian *Sun* newspaper in May 2011, an anonymous ex-PLAN combatant said in a letter hand-delivered to the paper that he felt that the Namibian people deserved the truth about Cassinga. The writer supports the contention that SWAPO had obtained information of the impending attack on Cassinga, probably through the offices of Dieter Gerhardt. This also supports the contention that SWAPO command saw the attack on Cassinga as an opportunity to rid itself of the remnants of the Shipanga faction which SWAPO had transferred to Cassinga from Zambia shortly before the attack: "We are questioning the extent of culpable negligence on the part of the SWAPO leadership because we have concrete evidence that SWAPO's military intelligence had foreknowledge of the impending attack and had notified the movement's leadership, yet nothing was done either to protect the refugees and minimize death or even evacuate the refugees to a safer place."

The writer also questions how the information was passed on, as well as the unreliable numbers of casualties quoted by SWAPO: "People are talking how SWAPO sources inside Namibia allegedly transmitted the information via our representatives in Europe, who in turn informed the SWAPO leadership in Angola. We want to know whether that is true or not. If true, then, we have the right to know why nothing was done to protect the refugees." He also questions the "fluctuating number" of those killed in the Cassinga massacre: "In the past we were told about 600 people died, but this year the NBC placed the number at over one thousand."

We have here a picture being painted of an entirely dishonest SWAPO high command. Each person questioning SWAPO's decisions and motives can see the web of untruth spun by the organization, but are unable to see the whole picture. The sad fact is that SWAPO cynically played their own people, as well as well-meaning foreigners, in a complex political game that subverted the nature of the United Nations humanitarian organs—the UNHCR and UNICEF—who were hoodwinked into supplying SWAPO guerrilla camps disguised as refugee camps, but also used the information of impending attacks to rid themselves of inconvenient cadres within the movement who were questioning Nujoma's motives and integrity at the time.

To further ram home the truth about Cassinga, some excerpts from a newly revealed source follow. One of the paratroopers in the Cassinga attack, Jan Volschenk, found a soldier's notebook among the ruins of the barrack buildings. He showed it to his superior officer who had a quick look and told him it was of little value. This, of course, was before the deluge of Soviet and SWAPO propaganda descended upon the Cassinga victors' heads when they returned home. Volschenk kept the notebook as a memento and forgot about it for more than 30 years. When the author appealed to any paratroopers for any information about the battle, Volschenk remembered the little notebook and asked whether the author was interested in reading it. The contents are a revelation and a summary is presented below, spelling and grammar verbatim:

ZAMBIAN SCHOLAR'S EXERCISE BOOK
Subject: Political Education
Name: Namana
School: Adult School
Place: Moscow T Camp
Date:

Comrade Absalom Nabot Namana Tomothy
Moscow Training Camp
R.P. de Angola
POLITIC BOOK SWAPO OF NAMIBIA

Administration in Moscow

1. Camp Comittee Camp Commander
2. Disciplinary Comittee Commissars
3. Subcomittee Teacher Brigade Instructors
4. Branch Comitee Detachment Com

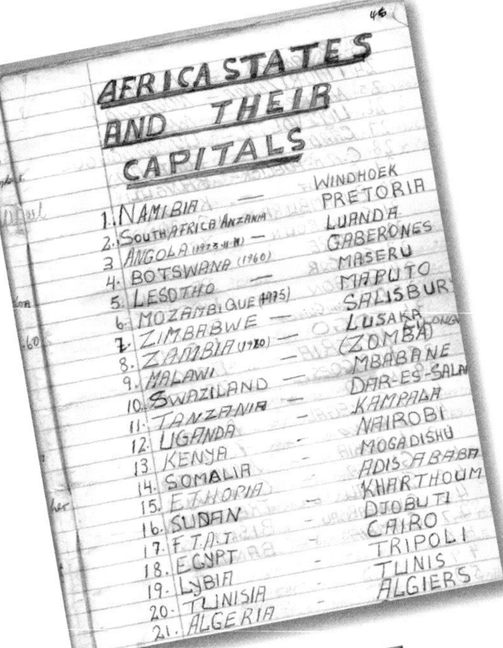

AFRICA STATES AND THEIR CAPITALS

1. NAMIBIA — WINDHOEK
2. SOUTH AFRICA AZANIA — PRETORIA
3. ANGOLA — LUANDA
4. BOTSWANA (1966) — GABERONES
5. LESOTHO — MASERU
6. MOZAMBIQUE (1975) — MAPUTO
7. ZIMBABWE — SALISBURY
8. ZAMBIA — LUSAKA
9. MALAWI — (ZOMBA)
10. SWAZILAND — MBABANE
11. TANZANIA — DAR-ES-SALAAM
12. UGANDA — KAMPALA
13. KENYA — NAIROBI
14. SOMALIA — MOGADISHU
15. ETHOPIA — ADIS ABABA
16. SUDAN — KHARTHOUM
17. F.T.A.I. — DJOBUTI
18. EGYPT — CAIRO
19. LYBIA — TRIPOLI
20. TUNISIA — TUNIS
21. ALGERIA — ALGIERS

STUFF BOARDS IN MOSCOW
Adminstratieve Bodies:

Campcomittee

1. Highest and have the authority of all functions and power of the campcomittees.
2. Direct and control the actions of all cadres.
3. It shall have a power to dissolve remove all members in the camp.
4. It makes laws of the camp.
5. All officers and departments must be answerable. The minets must reach the c sec before 48h00.
6. The campcomittee will be answerable solery the action of CHQ.
7. The officers member of campcomittee cannot be arrested without warned from the camp commander unless for extraordinary reason.

Subcomittee

Brigade Commander is a Chairman
Gathers two times in each month. It is a committee contacting camp com and cadres. One of the political instructor Secr.
It has the authority to dismiss Detachment C, Platoon C or Platoon.
It has a right to point Detachmnet C Platoon C
Their minets must be brought to the camp secretary
The Subcomittee is under control of the Campcomittee.

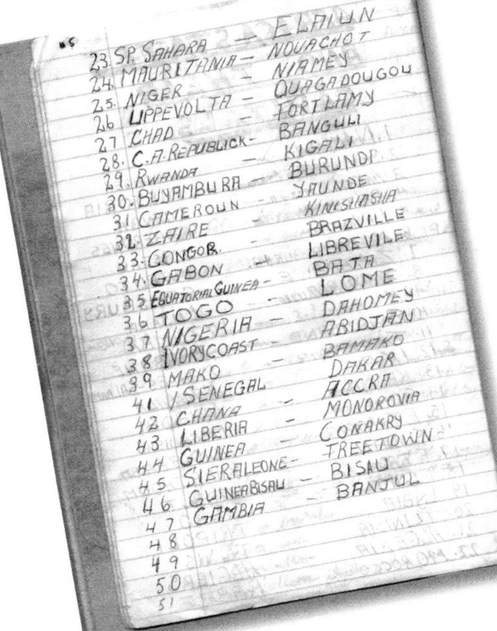

23. SP. SAHARA — ELAIUN
24. MAURITANIA — NOUACHOT
25. NIGER — NIAMEY
26. UPPEVOLTA — OUAGADOUGOU
27. CHAD — FORT LAMY
28. C.A. REPUBLICK — BANGULI
29. RWANDA — KIGALI
30. BUYAMBURA — BURUNDI
31. CAMEROUN — YAUNDE
32. ZAIRE — KINISHASHA
33. CONGO — BRAZVILLE
34. GABON — LIBREVILLE
35. EQUATORIAL GUINEA — BATA
36. TOGO — LOME
37. NIGERIA — DAHOMEY
38. IVORYCOAST — ABIDJAN
39. MAKO — BAMAKO
41. SENEGAL — DAKAR
42. GHANA — ACCRA
43. LIBERIA — MONOROVIA
44. GUINEA — CONAKRY
45. SIERALEONE — TREETOWN
46. GUINEABISAU — BISAU
47. GAMBIA — BANJUL
48.
49.
50.
51.

Branch Committee

Chairman Detachment Commander
Despute of Detachment Commander is Secr.
They gather every time they get a problem.
Members are Section, Platoon Detachment Commanders.

Camp officers and their responsibilities

1. Camp Commander Nolikonkole
   He/she rules all (detachments) departments.
   A chairman of camp committee.
   Chief Director of all departments.
   A bridge between camp and CHQ
   Can dismiss and appoint an officer
   An organizer of guarding
   With commissars make good orders in the camp
   He can break the deadlock in the camp meeting

2. Discipline Commander or Camp Political Commissioner Shafewange Nghilundwa
   Director of political activities in camp
   Camp Commissar is chief adviser to Camp Commander
   He is a bridge (reporter) between camp office and CHQ
   Check the morals and discipline in the camp
   It is his/her responsibility to convince the cadres in discipline, moral and politic.
   He/she is a discipline commander
   Chairman of Disciplinary Committee.
   He must bring good contact between the cadres and masses.
   He/she has authority to visit the jail and convince the prisoners.
   He/she is responsibility to inform the peoples someone crime and punishment.
   He/she is chief adviser of womans council.
   He/she is under control of camp Commander.

3. Camp Secretary Moxs
   He/she is a Secretary of Camp Committee.
   He invites the congress before two days 48h00 he must also invite the member of CHQ
   C Secretary and C Commander select the minets to be discussed in a C Comittee congress.
   He keep the reporters (issues) of the camp.
   He makes good order and camporder.
   He must charge the corresponding letters
   Camp Secre and C Commander make good administrative
   He writes the recruits and soldiers who go for training.

4. Security Officer Muchona Mahwilile
   He represent the camp security
   He is responsibility to charge all people come in the camp.
   He is a chairman of security and introcation.
   He/she is responsibility to find the traitors and puppets.

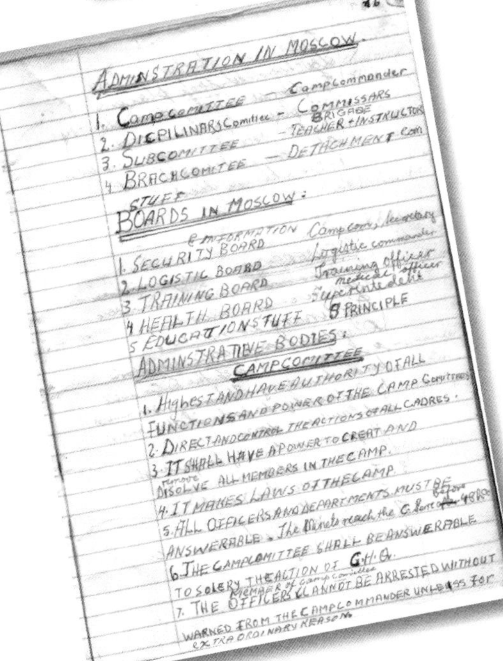

ADMINSTRATION IN MOSCOW.

1. Campcomittee — Campcommander
2. DICPILINARY Comittee — COMMISSARS
3. SUBCOMITTEE — BRIGADE TEACHER + INSTRUCTOR
4. BRACHCOMITEE — DETACHMENT Com

STUFF BOARDS IN MOSCOW:

1. SECURITY & INFORMATION BOARD — Camp com, Secretary
2. LOGISTIC BOARD — Logistic commander
3. TRAINING BOARD — Training officer
4. HEALTH BOARD — medical officer
5. EDUCATION STUFF — Superintedent & PRINCIPLE

ADMINSTRATIVE BODIES:

CAMPCOMITTEE

1. Highest AND HAVE AUTHORITY OF ALL FUNCTIONS AND POWER OF THE CAMP Comittees
2. DIRECT AND CONTROL THE ACTIONS OF ALL CADRES.
3. IT SHALL HAVE A POWER TO CREAT AND DISOLVE remove ALL MEMBERS IN THE CAMP.
4. IT MAKES LAWS OF THE CAMP.
5. ALL OFFICERS AND DEPARTMENTS MUST BE ANSWERABLE. The Minets reach the C. Secr before 48h00
6. THE CAMPCOMITTEE SHALL BE ANSWERABLE TO SOLERY THE ACTION OF C.H.Q.
7. THE OFFICERS Member of Camp comittee CANNOT BE ARRESTED WITHOUT WARNED FROM THE CAMPCOMMANDER UNLESS FOR EXTRAORDINARY REASON.

He keep the prisoners and criminals.
He advise Co Commander about camp security.
He charges the recruits.
He is the leader of Military Police.
He must find out that P. M. gets politics, tactics, studies.
Each lost missing in the camp ammunition and weapon must be reported to him.
He is responsibility for charging (mistakes) accident done in the camp.
In his actions he must have contact with the C Commander.
He must report all events to the C Commander monthly

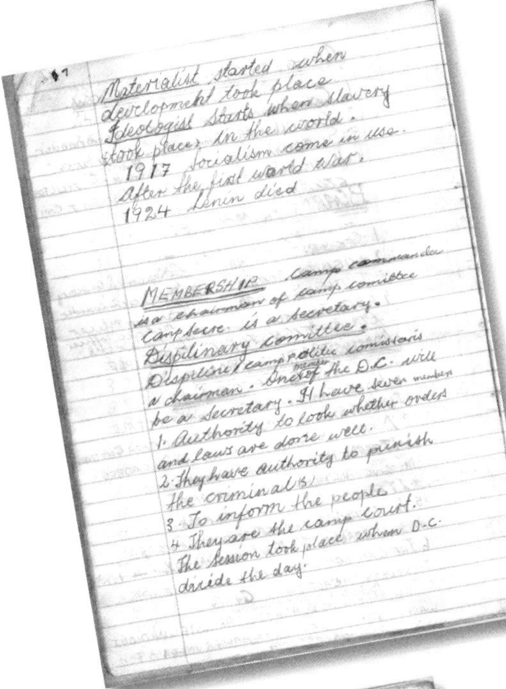
Materialist started when
development took place
Ideologist starts when slavery
took place. In the world.
1917 socialism come in use.
After the first world war.
1924 Lenin died

MEMBERSHIP Camp commander
is a chairman of camp comittee
camp secre. is a secretary.
Displinary comittee.
Dispiline / camp politic comissaris
a chairman. One of the D.C. member will
be a secretary. It have seven members
1. Authority to look whether orders
and laws are done well.
2. They have authority to punish
the criminal(s)
3. To inform the people
4 They are the camp court.
The session took place when D.C.
decide the day.

5. Logistic officer Mbalaganja German Africa
He receive all things in the camp and note them in the book.
He divide things among the people according to the need.
He must report the used of the things.
He must keep the things in the right way.
He must be ordered by C Commander to give things.
He must be in a good contact with C Commander.

6. Medical Health Officer Dr. Kalangula
He must keep the health of peoples.
He must see that the ill peoples are treated well.
He is responsibility for camp cleaniness.
He advise the logistic officer.
He advise the training officer that the recruit is in good health to go for training.
He must give the report to c Commander.
He advises the women.

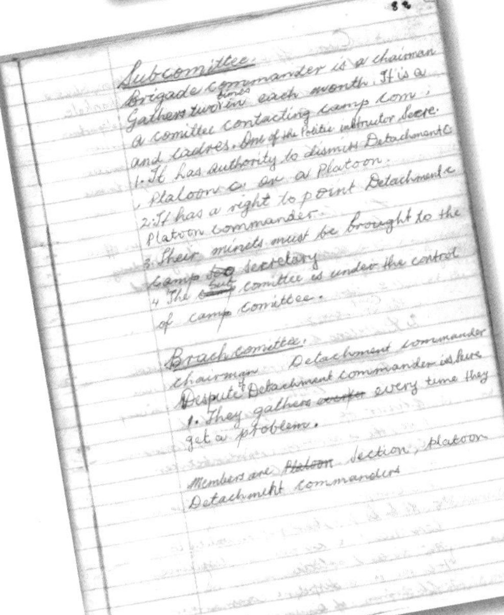
Subcomittee.
Brigade commander is a chairman
Gathers two times in each month. It is a
a comittee contacting camp com.
and cadres. One of the Politic instructor secre.
1. It has authority to dismiss Detachment C
Platoon c. or a Platoon.
2. It has a right to point Detachment c
Platoon commander.
3. Their minds must be brought to the
camp sub secretary
4 The sub comittee is under the control
of camp comittee.

Brach comittee. Detachment commander
chairman Detachment commander is here
Despute of Detachment every time they
1. They gathers
get a problem.

Members are Section, platoon
Detachment commanders

7. Brigade Commander Nomuxwika
He must know that the soldiers are ready to combat.
He is the head of all military activities.
Next C Commander.
He must know that all soldiers are present in the camp.
He give the work to peoples in the camp with contacting C Commander.
With C Commander and Security officer make arrangements of camp safety.
With superintendent he give the sleep place.
He must know how many guns are at the detachment.
He must do the lol call.
He is under the control of C Commander

8. Training Officer Comr. Couaya
He is ready to give a moral of combat among the fighters.
He chose the leader of military activities.
He must see to it that the soldiers are trained well in physical and tactic training.
He is the leader of the whole system of military training.
All detachment commander are under his control and he reports the event to C Commander.
He must know the Militants behavior.
He reports the progress in military training.
He has connection with C Commander.

9. Technical Officer Comr. Nghimanundowa Hafami
Give advise to the logistic to keep the guns.

10. Superintendent. Comr. Davy Haikali
He is the highcare-taker of places in the camp.
He must take care of guests
It is her responsible to look for places (dirty or clean).
He work in connection with camp commander.

11. Deputies. Aapetha

[The following section in capital letters has been translated from the Oshiwambo Kwanyama dialect]

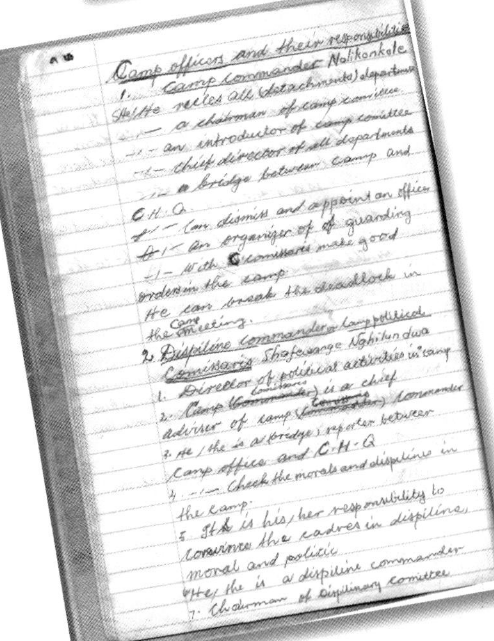
Camp officers and their responsibilities
1. Camp commander Nalikonkole
She/He reeles all (detachments) departments
-/- a chairman of camp comittee
-/- an introductor of camp comittee
-/- chief director of all departments
-/- a bridge between camp and
C.H.Q.
-/- Can dismiss and appoint an officer
-/- An organizer of guarding
-/- With comissaris make good
orders in the camp
He can break the deadlock in
the camp meeting.
2. Dispiline commander or Camp political
Comissaris Shafewange Nghilundwa
1. Director of political activities in camp
2. Camp comissaris is a chief
adviser of camp commander
3. He / she is a bridge, reporter between
camp office and C.H.Q
4. -/- Check the morals and dispiline in
the camp.
5. It is his/her responsibility to
convince the cadres in dispiline,
moral and politic
6. He/she is a dispiline commander
7. Chairman of Dispilinary comittee

DEPUTIES: SOMEBODY WHO REPRESENTS ON BEHALF OF. THEY ARE EXPECTED TO PERFORM THE DUTIES OF THE COMMANDING OFFICER WHEN HE/SHE IS NOT AVAILABLE.

EXAMPLE: WHEN THE BRIGADE COMMANDER IS NOT THERE THEN THE DEPUTY WILL TAKE OVER THE COMMANDER'S RESPONSIBILITIES UNTIL HE/SHE RETURNS. DEPUTIES CAN BE A MEMBERS OF THE
SUB-COMMITEE.
THE CAMP COMMANDER'S DEPUTY IS ALSO A MEMBER OF THE COMMITTEE IN THE BASE BUT HAS NOT BEEN NOMINATED.

BASE COMMITTEE: THE BASE COMMITTEE CAN NOMINATE OR APPOINT ANY MEMBER FROM THE BASE DUE TO HIS/HER

KNOWLEDGE AND EXPERIENCE .
CHQ HAVE THE RIGHT TO APPOINT A MEMBER AS A PERMANENT MEMBER OF THE COMMITTEE. IT WILL BE THE RESPONSIBILITY OF THE CHAIRPERSON TO INFORM CHQ OF ANY MEETINGS.

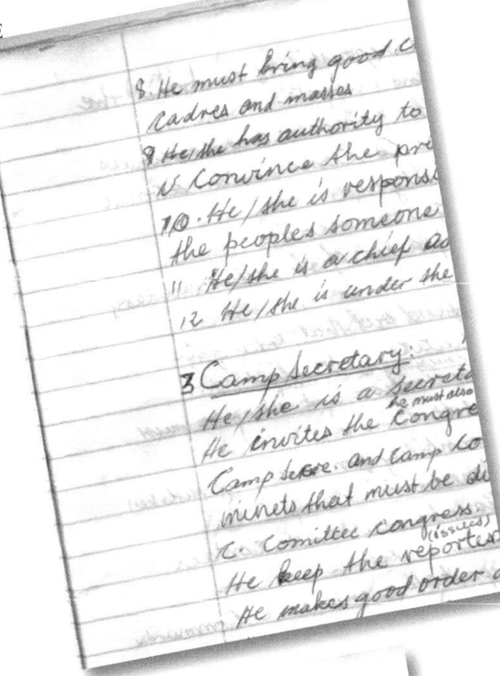

8. He must bring good c
cadres and masses
9 He/she has authority to
convince the pr
10. He/she is responsi
the peoples someone
11 He/she is a chief ad
12 He/she is under the

3 Camp Secretary:
He/she is a secreta he must also
He invites the Congre
Camp score and Camp Co
minets that must be di
C. Comitee congress. (issues)
He keep the reporter
He makes good order a

<u>RELATIONS OF OFFICIALS</u>:

1. RESPECT
2. NOT UNDERMINING THE WORK OF ANOTHER OFFICIAL
3. TEAM WORK
4. GUIDING/ADVISING EACH OTHER
5. TRY NOT TO BOAST IN YOUR WORK AND TO DISRESPECT OTHERS
6. NOT TO MISMANAGE FUNDS

SWAPO OF NAMIBIA
Structure
National Organs
SWAPO Congress 5 years
Central Committee (45 members) Yearly
National Executive Committee (once a month) (17)
SWAPO Youth League
Elders Council

Wings
PLAN
SWAPO Womans Council

Reginal Organs
RC once every two year.
REC once in three months

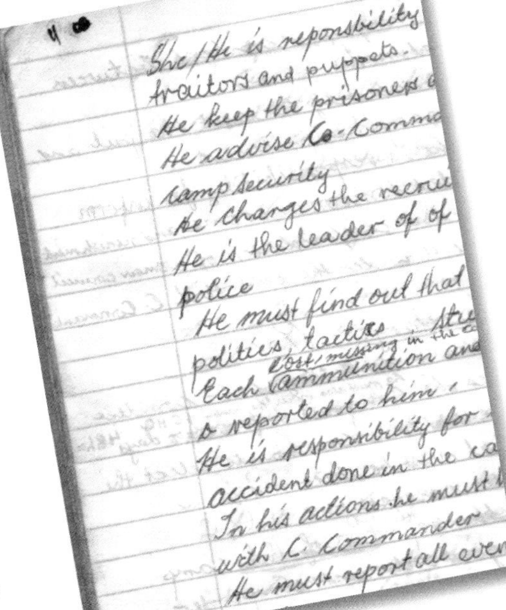

She/He is reponsbility
traitors and puppets.
He keep the prisoners
He advise Co-Comma
camp security
He charges the recrui
He is the leader of of
police
He must find out that
politics tactics lost/missing in the
Each ammunition and
a reported to him
He is responsibility for
accident done in the ca
In his actions he must
with C. Commander
He must report all even

District Organs
ADC meet annually
DEC once a year

Branch Organs
BAC meet annually
BEC once a month recruits

Wings of the Organization
Peoples Liberation Army of Namibia PLAN
SWAPO Youth League
SWAPO Womens Council
SWAPO Elders Council

Members of Central Committee
They are 45 for Namibia. Members meet yearly.
Tasks of CC. They are highest body between congress, to adopt resolutions, descisions, convene congress, promoting political ed,
Power to expel member of organization, revenues and disburse funds and properties of organization:

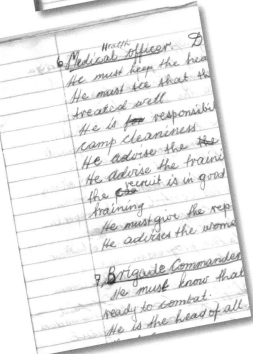

President. Sem Nuayoma
Vice President. Mishake Muyongo
National Chairman. David Meroro
Administrative Secketary. Moses Garoeb
Secretary for Defense. Peter Nanyemba
Acting Secretary for Foreign Relations. Peter Mweshihange
Acting Secretary for Labor. John Otto
Member of Military Council. Dimo Amambo
Political Commisar of PLAN. Greenwell Matongo
Deputy Secretary of Defence. Richard Kapelwa
Acting organizing secretary. Homateni Kalwenya
Representative to Americans and UN. Theo Ben Gurirab
Member of Military Council. Jackson H. Ndandi
Assistant director UN Institute for Namibia. Hidipo Hamutenga
General Treasurer. Lucas Pohamba
Member of NEC. Ewald Katjwena
Director SWAPO radio programme. Vinia Ndadi
Deputy Dir for health and social welfare. Mrs. Dr. Libertine Amadhila
Acting Secr. for Information and Publicity. Peter Katjavivi
Secretary for Legal affairs. Ernest Tjajiriange
Director of UN Institute for Namibia. Gotfried Geingob
Acting Secretary of Transport. Maxton Joseph
Chairman of SWAPO Elders Council. Simon S. Kaukungua
Deputy Chairman of SWAPO. E.C. Jackson Mazazi
Assistant Secr. for Foreign Affairs. Heuanwa Sheepo

Acting Secr. for Economic Affairs. Ben Amadhila.
Member of SWAPO Womans Council. Mrs. Putse Appolus
Member of SWAPO Womans Council. Bejamin Namahambo
Secretary of YL. Luli Hivelwa
Acting secr. for Education and Culture. Ninekela Kalenga
Secr. to the Presidency. Kapuka Nauyale
Secr. for Health and Social Welfare. Dr. Iango Indongo
Member of Military Council. Solomon Hewala
Member of Military Council. Nickey Iambo
Director of Namibian Ed. and Health Centre. Helmut Angula
Assistant Secr. for Information and Publicity. Jesaya Njamu
Member of Central Committee. Sam Musialela
Member of Central Committee. Mrs. N. Mavulu
Member of Central Committee. Mrs Agnella Agwala
Member of Central Committee. Lemmy Matengu
Deputy Secr. of SWAPO Youth League (represent us in Tjeko Slovakia). Tomas N Komati
Secretary of SWAPO Youth League. [two names crossed out]

As can be seen in this humble soldier's notebook, Cassinga, or Moscow Training Camp, was a well-organized military training camp in the Soviet tradition. It puts paid to SWAPO's decades-long subterfuge which deceived western nations and enabled SWAPO to enjoy the support and protection of the United Nations while they pursued their war of terror on the civilian inhabitants of Namibia/South West Africa.

That SWAPO disguised their military camps as refugee camps was yet another example of the disregard the organization felt for humanitarian norms. That they cold-bloodedly filled the camps with their own abducted countryfolk, exposing them to danger, disease and trauma, is something that should attract the ire of the civilized world. Instead, a veil of silence has been drawn over the facts, ignored by the sponsors of the liberation fighters. Perhaps it is a case of terrorism really working for its perpetrators. Those who should complain about the misuse of their trust and goodwill are in fact terrified to do so.

That the South Africans were concerned by the possible presence of civilians in the base is reflected in the TRC record:

> The SADF's anxiety about external reaction is reflected in a signal from the chief of the defence force, sent at 19h30, enquiring whether any women and children had been killed. This took priority over a 20h50 signal enquiring whether any Cubans had been captured. In response to the earlier query, SWA Tactical Headquarters sent out a top-secret message that night (OPS/104/04) reporting that there were many women and children at Alpha and that large numbers had been killed. Among the dead women, the message reported, many had been in uniform and many in the trenches.
> —*The South African Truth and Reconciliation Commission Vol 2*, Chapter 2, 'The State Outside South Africa between 1960–1990'

AFTERWORD

That the battle of Cassinga was so controversial in so many of its attributes perhaps signifies its importance to all the sides involved. To SWAPO it was a grievous blow to their ambitions to engulf South West Africa by force of arms just prior to democratic elections in that country. To the Republic of South Africa, it was a signal to SWAPO as well as the international community that, despite the very damaging propaganda which was bound to follow such a bold attack into Angola, they were prepared to take the pressure if it meant that the communist-inspired SWAPO leadership would be stopped in their tracks. It was also perhaps meant as a showcase for a South African Defence Force that was almost totally self-reliant; despite comprehensive arms sanctions and embargoes, this military power was a warning to the USSR and its surrogate Cuba, to curb their ambitions in Africa.

To Cuba, Cassinga yielded the largest loss of troops in a single day in its entire African adventure. In the grand scheme of things, the Cuban loss was incidental to the battle in that they and FAPLA simply came to the aid of their allies and suffered greatly for it, without gaining or losing any strategic advantage.

For FAPLA and the MPLA, Cassinga was a strong warning that South Africa had the wherewithal to strike hard and quickly at leisure into the heartland of Angola.

*****

For those from all sides who fought and perished at Cassinga, the immortal words of the memorial at Kohima in India are appropriate:

"When you go home, tell them of us and say, for their tomorrow, we gave our today."

APPENDIX I: THE T-10 PARACHUTE SYSTEM

The T-10 parachute system is a series of static line-deployed parachutes used by many armed forces for mass-assault combat airborne operations and training. The most current version is the T-10D which is currently being replaced by the T-11 parachute system.

Depending upon air density and the jumper's total weight, the parachute's average rate of descent is between 22 to 24 feet per second (6.7 to 7.3m/s); total suspended weight limitation is 360 pounds (160kg). The parachute is deployed using either a 15 or 20 foot (4.6 or 6.1m) static line, allowing the parachutist to be delivered by either C-130 or C-17 aircraft. The T-10D main parachute is a parabolic-shape and has a nominal diameter of 35 feet (11m), 30 suspension lines and a mesh anti-inversion net.

The T-10D parachute assembly consists of five components: pack tray, troop harness, deployment bag, riser and canopy. The parachute has a combined service life of 16.5 years; service life is 12 years and shelf life is 4.5 years. The T-10D parachute must be repacked every 120 days. The T-10D parachute is made of nylon materials commonly used in the manufacturing of parachutes.

The harness has integral D-rings which serve to anchor the reserve parachute as well as the weapons container, which is released to hang beneath the paratrooper once his main parachute has deployed.

The release mechanisms are: a quick-jettison system to enable the paratrooper to jettison his weapons container in an emergency and two Capewell release clips on the shoulders for each of the riser groups attached to the harness. One or both of these are released in event of a water landing or if the paratrooper is being dragged by wind after landing. A quick-release box with a safety pin is used to allow the whole harness to fall away once it is activated.

A belly-band, which is a fabric belt with a buckle which straps the main container to the body of the paratrooper, allows the paratrooper to fasten a weapon to his side without the need to use a weapons container.

APPENDIX II: WEAPONS USED AT THE BATTLE OF CASSINGA

Light Machine Gun (LMG)
also known as FN MAG SADF

Designer	Ernest Vervier
Designed	1950s
Manufacturer	Fabrique Nationale (FN)
Produced	1958–present
Specifications	
Weight	11.79 kg (25.99 lb)
Length	1,263 mm (49.7 in)
Barrel **length**	630 mm (24.8 in)
Width	118.7 mm (4.7 in)
Height	263 mm (10.4 in)
Cartridge	7.62×51mm NATO
Action	Gas-operated, open bolt
Rate of fire	650–1,000 rpm
Muzzle velocity	840 m/s (2,756 ft/s)
Effective range	800 m
Maximum range	1,500 m from tripod
Feed system	Non-disintegrating DM1 or disintegrating M13 linked belt
Sights	Folding leaf sight with aperture and notch, front blade

RPD Light Machine Gun
SWAPO/ Cuba/FAPLA

Designer	Vasily Degtyaryov
Designed	1943–1944
Variants	RPDM, Type 56, Type 56-1, Type 62
Specifications	
Weight	6.6 kg (14.55 lb)
Length	1,037 mm (40.8 in)
Barrel **length**	520 mm (20.5 in)
Cartridge	7.62x39mm
Action	Gas-operated
Rate of fire	650-750 rpm
Muzzle velocity	735 m/s (2,411 ft/s)
Effective range	100–1,000 m sight adjustments
Feed system	Non-disintegrating 100-round segmented belt stored in a drum container
Sights	Open-type sights with rear sliding notch and semi-hooded front post, 596.6 mm (23.5 in) sight radius

R1 Folding Butt
also known as FN FAL SADF

Designer	Dieudonné Saive, Ernest Vervier
Designed	1947–1953
Manufacturer	Fabrique Nationale (FN)
Produced	1953–present
Number built	> 2,000,000
Variants	11
Specifications	
Weight	FAL 50.61: 3.90 kg (8.6 lb)
Length	FAL 50.61 (stock extended): 1,095 mm (43.1 in) FAL 50.61 (stock folded): 845 mm (33.3 in)
Barrel **length**	FAL 50.61: 533 mm (21.0 in)
Cartridge	7.62x51mm NATO
Action	Gas-operated, tilting breechblock
Rate of fire	650–700 rpm
Muzzle velocity	FAL 50.61: 840 m/s (2,755.9 ft/s)
Effective range	200–600 m sight adjustments
Feed system	20 or 30-round detachable box magazine
Sights	Aperture rear sight, post front sight; sight radius FAL 50.61: 549 mm (21.6 in)

M26 Hand Grenade
SADF

In service	1950s–1970s
Used by	United States, Israel, United Kingdom, Australia, Canada, Portugal, South Africa
Wars	Vietnam , Falklands
Specifications	
Weight	454 g
Length	99 mm
Diameter	57 mm
Filling	Composition B
Filling weight	164 g
Detonation mechanism	Timed Friction Fuse

F1 Hand Grenade
SWAPO/Cuba/FAPLA

Weight	600 g
Length	130 mm
Diameter	55 mm
Filling	Trinitrotoluene
Filling weight	60 g

AK-47 Assault Rifle
SWAPO/Cuba/FAPLA

Designer	Mikhail Kalashnikov
Designed	1944–1946
Manufacturer	Izhmash
Number built	>75 million AK-47s >100 million AK-type rifles
Variants	14
Specifications	
Weight	4.3 kg (9.5 lb) with empty magazine
Length	870 mm (34.3 in) fixed wooden stock 875 mm (34.4 in) folding stock extended 645 mm (25.4 in) stock folded
Barrel **length**	415 mm (16.3 in)
Cartridge	7.62x39mm M43/M67
Action	Gas-operated, rotating bolt
Rate of fire	600 rpm
Muzzle velocity	715 m/s (2,346 ft/s)
Effective range	300 m (330 yd) full automatic 400 m (440 yd) semi-automatic
Feed system	10-, 20-, 30-, 40- or 75-round detachable box and drum-style magazine, also compatible with 40-round box or 75-round drum magazines from the RPK
Sights	Adjustable iron sights, 100–800 m adjustments, 378 mm (14.9 in) sight radius

AKM / AKMS (Folding Stock) Assault Rifle
SWAPO/Cuba/FAPLA

Designer	Mikhail Kalashnikov
Designed	1950s
Number built	10,278,300
Variants	AKMS, AKMP, AKML, AKMLP, AKMSP, AKMSU, AKMSN, AKMSNP
Specifications	
Weight	AKM: 3.1 kg (6.83 lb) AKMS: 3.3 kg (7.3 lb)
Length	AKM, AKML: 880 mm (34.6 in) AKMS, AKMSN: 902 mm (35.5 in) stock extended / 655 mm (25.8 in) stock folded
Barrel **length**	415 mm (16.3 in)
Cartridge	7.62x39mm
Action	Gas operated, rotating bolt
Rate of fire	600 rpm
Muzzle velocity	715 m/s (2,346 ft/s)
Effective range	400 m,100–1,000 m sight adjustments
Maximum range	1000 m
Feed system	20 or 30-round detachable box magazine, also compatible with 40-round box or 75-round drum magazines from the RPK
Sights	Rear sight notch on sliding tangent, front post. Sight radius: 378 mm (14.9 in)

SKS Rifle

SWAPO/Cuba/FAPLA

Designer	Sergei Gavrilovich Simonov
Designed	1944
Number built	15,000,000
Variants	Chinese Type 56, Yugoslavian PAP, Romanian SKS, Albanian SKS, East German SKS, (North) Vietnamese SKS, North Korean SKS
Specifications	
Weight	3.85 kg (8 lb 8 oz)
Length	1,021 mm (40.2 in), M59/66: 1,117 mm (44.0 in)
Barrel **length**	521 mm (20.5 in) M59/66: 558.8 mm (22.00 in)
Cartridge	7.62x39mm
Action	Short-stroke gas piston, tilting bolt, self-loading
Rate of fire	Semi-automatic
Muzzle velocity	735 m/s (2,410 ft/s)
Effective range	400 m (440 yd)
Feed system	10-round internal box magazine, 10-round stripper clip-fed or individual round loading
Sights	Hooded post front sight, tangent notch rear sight to 1,000 m

UZI Hand-Machine Carbine

SADF

Designer	Uziel Gal
Designed	1948
Manufacturer	Israel Military Industries, FN Herstal, Norinco, Lyttleton Engineering Works (under Vektor Arms), RH-ALAN
Produced	1950–present
Number built	>10,000,000
Variants	5
Specifications	
Weight	3.5 kg (7.72 lb)
Length	640 mm (25.2 in) stock extended 470 mm (18.5 in) stock collapsed
Barrel **length**	260 mm (10.2 in)
Cartridge	9x19mm Parabellum, .22 LR, .45 ACP, .41 AE
Action	Blowback
Rate of fire	600 rpm
Muzzle velocity	400 m/s
Effective range	200 m
Feed system	10- (.22 and .41 AE), 16- (.45 ACP), 20-, 32-, 40- and 50-round box magazines
Sights	Iron sights

RPG-7 Rocket Propelled Grenade

SADF/SWAPO/Cuba/FAPLA

Manufacturer	Bazalt, Defense Industries Organization
Unit cost	US$3,000
Designed	June 1961
Variants	RPG-7V2 (current model) Current production ammunition for the RPG-7V2 consists of four types: PG-7VL standard HEAT warhead for most vehicles and fortified targets (93 mm) PG-7VR dual HEAT warhead for defeating modern heavily armoured vehicles equipped with reactive armour (105 mm) TBG-7V thermobaric warhead for anti-personnel and urban warfare (105 mm) OG-7V fragmentation warhead for anti-personnel warfare (within calibre due to limitations of international treaties)
Specifications	
Weight	7 kg (15 lb)
Length	950 mm (37.4 in)
Calibre	85 mm
Muzzle velocity	115 m/s
Maximum range	920 m (1,000 yd) (self detonates)
Sights	PGO-7 (2.7x)

B10 Recoilless Rifle

SWAPO/Cuba/FAPLA

Designer	KBM (Kolomna)
Variants	Type 65
Specifications	
Weight	85.3 kg (188 lbs)
Length	1.85 m (6 ft) travel position
Barrel **length**	1.660 mm
Calibre	82 mm
Action	Single shot
Carriage	Two wheeled with integrated tripod
Elevation	-20/+35°
Traverse	250° in each direction for 360° total
Rate of fire	5 to 7 rpm
Effective range	400 m (437 yd)
Maximum range	4,500 m (4,921 yd)
Feed system	Breech loaded
Sights	Optical (PBO-2)

PPSh Sub-Machine Gun

SWAPO/Cuba/FAPLA

Designer	Georgi Shpagin
Manufacturer	Numerous
Designed	1941
Number built	> 6,000,000
Variants	4
Specifications	
Weight	3.63 kg (8 lb) (without magazine)
Length	843 mm (33.2 in)
Barrel **length**	269 mm (10.6 in)
Cartridge	7.62x25mm Tokarev
Action	Blowback, open bolt
Rate of fire	900 rpm
Muzzle velocity	488 m/s (1,600.6 ft/s)
Effective range	150 m
Feed system	35-round box magazine or 71-round drum magazine

KPV 14.5mm 4-Barrelled Heavy Machine Gun

SWAPO/Cuba/FAPLA

Designed	1944
Specifications	
Weight	52.2 kg (115.08 lb)
Length	1,980 mm (78 in)
Barrel **length**	1,346 mm (53.0 in) x 4
Width	162 mm
Height	225 mm
Cartridge	14.5×114mm
Calibre	14.5 mm
Action	Short recoil operation
Rate of fire	550–600 rpm
Muzzle velocity	1,005 m/s
Effective range	2,000m ground, 1,500 air
Maximum range	4,000 m
Feed system	40-round belt
Sights	iron or optical

60mm Patrol Mortar (Patmor)

SADF

Designer	Edgar Brandt
Specifications	
Weight	19.05 kg (42.0 lb)
Barrel **length**	726 mm (28.6 in)
Shell	1.33 kg (2.94 lb)
Calibre	60 mm (2.36 in)
Elevation	+40° to +85°
Traverse	7°
Rate of fire	18 rpmute
Muzzle velocity	158 m/s (518 ft/s)
Maximum range	1815 m (1985 yd)

82mm Mortar

SWAPO/Cuba/FAPLA

Designed	1940–41
Produced	1941–43
Specifications	
Weight	56 kg (steel barrel)
Length	120 cm
Crew	4
Calibre	82 mm
Elevation	45°–85°
Traverse	5°–25° (using traversing mechanism)
Rate of fire	15–25 rpm
Sights	MPB-82

No. 8 Landmine

SADF

Specifications	
Diameter	259 mm
Height	175 mm
Weight	7.4 kg explosive content: 7 kg of a 60/40 RDX/ TNT mix
Operating pressure	150–220 kg

ZPU 14.5 Anti-Aircraft Gun

SWAPO/Cuba/FAPLA

Model	ZPU-1	ZPU-2 (early)	ZPU-2 (late)	ZPU-4
Barrels	1	2	2	4
Weight (travelling)	413 kg (910 lb)	994 kg (2,191 lb)	649 kg (1,430 lb)	1,810 kg (3,990 lb)
Weight (firing)	413 kg (910 lb)	639 kg (1,408 lb)	621 kg (1,369 lb)	1,810 kg (3,990 lb)
Length (travel)	3.44 m (11.28 ft)	3.54 m (11.61 ft)	3.87 m (12.69 ft)	4.53 m (14.86 ft)
Width (travel)	1.62 m (5.31 ft)	1.92 m (6.29 ft)	1.37 m (4.49 ft)	1.72 m (5.64 ft)
Height (travel)	1.34 m (4.39 ft)	1.83 m (6.00 ft)	1.1 m (3.60 ft)	2.13 m (7 ft)
Elevation	+88/-8	+90/-7	+85/-15	+90/-10
Traverse	360			
Maximum range	8,000 m (8,749 yd)			
Maximum altitude	5,000 m (16,404 ft)			
Effective altitude	1,400 m (4,593 ft)			
Ammunition (rounds)	1200	2400		4800
Crew	4	5		

APPENDIX III: VEHICLES USED AT THE BATTLE OF CASSINGA

BMP Infantry Fighting Vehicle

SWAPO/Cuba/FAPLA

	BMP-1 (ob'yekt 765Sp1)	BMP-1 (ob'yekt 765Sp2)	BMP-1 (ob'yekt 765Sp3)	BMP-1P (ob'yekt 765Sp4/5)	BMP-1D	BMP-2	BMP-3
Weight (MT)	12.6	13.0	13.2	13.4	14.5	14.0	18.7
Crew	3+8					3+7	
Main gun	73 mm 2A28 Grom low-pressure smoothbore semi-automatic gun					30 mm 2A42 autocannon	100 mm 2A70 rifled automatic gun/missile-launcher 30 mm 2A72 autocannon
Machine gun(s)	7.62 mm PKT coaxial						3 × 7.62 mm PKT (1 coaxial, 2 bow mounted)
ATGM (NATO designation)	9M14 Malyutka (AT-3 Sagger) and variants			(AT-5 Spandrel) or 9M111 Fagot (AT-4 Spigot) and variants	9M14 Malyutka or 9M113 Konkurs or removed (on most vehicles)	9M113 Konkurs (AT-5 Spandrel) or 9M111 Fagot (AT-4 Spigot) and variants	9M117 Bastion (AT-10 Stabber)
Engine	UTD-20 6-cylinder 4-stroke V-shaped airless-injection water-cooled diesel developing 300 hp (224 kW) at 2,600 rpm					UTD-20S1 diesel developing 300 hp (224 kW) at 2,600 rpm	UTD-29M 10-cylinder diesel developing 500 hp (375 kW) at 2,600 rpm
Power to weight ratio hp/MT (kW/MT)	23.8 (17.8)	23.1 (17.2)	22.7 (17.0)	22.4 (16.7)	20.7 (15.5)	21.4 (16.0)	26.7 (20.0)

BRDM-1 with 12.7mm DsHK Heavy Machine Gun

SWAPO/Cuba/FAPLA

The BRDM-1 (also known as the BTR-40P) first appeared in 1959, and was in production until 1966. Total production was around 10,000 vehicles; less than 600 remain in the reserves of a number of countries. It was armed with a pintle-mounted heavy machine gun. The initial version of the vehicle, the Model 1957, had an open roof, but the standard production model, the Model 1958, had a roof with twin hatches. The vehicle was used as the basis of the 2P27 anti-tank missile launcher, using AT-1 Snapper missiles mounted in a retractable launcher.

Iraqi BRDM-2

SWAPO/Cuba/FAPLA

The BRDM-2 was intended to replace the earlier BRDM-1 with a vehicle that had improved amphibious capabilities and better armament. The BRDM-2 is driven by a rear-mounted gasoline engine that also supplies power to a waterjet for amphibious travel. It has a crew of four: a driver, co-driver, commander, and gunner. The armament is the same as the BTR-60 armoured personnel carrier, a 14.5 mm KPV heavy machine gun with a 7.62 mm machine gun as a secondary weapon. The armour on the vehicle protects fully against small-arms fire and artillery shell splinters. This vehicle has been exported extensively and is in use in at least 45 countries. The BRDM-2 is sometimes confused with the Hungarian D-442 FUG amphibious scout car and the D-944 PSZH APC, which have rear engines but also have twin waterjets.

BTR 50

SWAPO/Cuba/FAPLA

Type	Amphibious Tracked Armoured Personnel Carrier
Place of origin	USSR
In service	1954–present
Designed	1952
Produced	1954–1970
Specifications	
Weight	14.5 MT
Length	7.08 m
Width	3.14 m
Height	2.03 m
Crew	2 (driver and commander) (+ 20 passengers)
Primary armament	None or 7.62 mm SGMB medium machine gun (BTR-50P) (1,250 rounds) 14.5 mm KPV heavy machine gun (BTR-50PA) 7.62 mm SGMB medium machine gun (BTR-50PK) (1,250 rounds)
Engine	V-6 6-cylinder 4-stroke in line water-cooled diesel 240 hp (179 kW) at 1,800 rpm
Power/weight	16.6 hp/t
Suspension	torsion bar
Ground clearance	370 mm
Fuel capacity	400 l
Operational range	400 km
Speed	44 km/h (road) 11 km/h (water)

T-34 Medium Tank

Cuba/FAPLA

Place of origin	USSR
In service	1940–present
Designer	T-34 Main Design Bureau (KMDB)
Designed	1937–40
Produced	1940– 58
Number built	84,070
Specifications	
Weight	26.5 MT (29.2 ST, 26.1 LT)
Length	6.68 m (21 ft 11 in)
Width	3 m (9 ft 10 in)
Height	2.45 m (8 ft)
Crew	4
Armour	16–60 mm turret, 15–47 mm hull
Primary armament	76.2 mm (3 in) F-34 tank gun
Secondary armament	2 ×7.62 mm (.308 in) DT machine guns
Engine	Model V-2 12-cyl diesel 500 hp (370 kW)
Power/weight	17.5 hp/MT
Suspension	Christie
Operational range	400 km (250 mi)
Speed	53 km/h (33 mph)

APPENDIX IV: SAAF AIRCRAFT USED AT THE BATTLE OF CASSINGA

Transall C-160 Heavy Transport Aircraft

General characteristics

Crew: 3 (2 pilots, flight engineer)

Capacity: 93 troops *or* 61–88 paratroops *or* 62 stretchers

Payload: 16,000 kg (35,275 lb)

Length: 32.40 m (106 ft 3½ in)

Wingspan: 40.00 m (131 ft 3 in)

Height: 11.65 m (38 ft 2¾ in)

Wing area: 160.0 m^2 (1,722 ft^2)

Empty weight: 29,000 kg (63,935 lb)

Max takeoff weight: 51,000 kg (112,435 lb)

Powerplant: 2 × Rolls-Royce Tyne Rty.20 Mk 22 turboprop, 4,549 kW (6,100 ehp) each

Performance

Never exceed speed: 593 km/h (320 knots, 368 mph)

Maximum speed: 513 km/h (277 knots, 319 mph) at 4,875 m (16,000 ft)

Stall speed: 177 km/h (95 knots, 110 mph) flaps down

Range: 1,853 km (1,000 nmi, 1,151 mi) with 16,000 kg payload, 30 min reserves

Ferry range: 8,858 km (4,780 nmi, 5,504 mi)

Service ceiling: 8,230 m (27,000 ft)

Rate of climb: 6.6 m/s (1,300 ft/min)

Wing loading: 319 kg/m^2 (65.3 lb/ft^2)

Power/mass: 0.18 kW/kg (0.11 hp/lb)

Lockheed C-130 Hercules Heavy Transport Aircraft

General characteristics

Crew: 5 (2 pilots, navigator, flight engineer and loadmaster)

Capacity: 92 passengers *or* 64 airborne troops *or* 74 litter patients with 2 medical personnel *or* 6 pallets *or* 2–3 HMMWVs *or* 2 M113 armoured personnel carrier

Payload: 45,000 lb (20,000 kg)

Length: 97 ft 9 in (29.8 m)

Wingspan: 132 ft 7 in (40.4 m)

Height: 38 ft 3 in (11.6 m)

Wing area: 1,745 ft^2 (162.1 m^2)

Empty weight: 75,800 lb (34,400 kg)

Useful load: 72,000 lb (33,000 kg)

Max takeoff weight: 155,000 lb (70,300 kg)

Powerplant: 4 × Allison T56-A-15 turboprops, 4,590 shp (3,430 kW) each

Performance

Maximum speed: 320 knots (366 mph, 592 km/h) at 20,000 ft (6,060 m)

Cruise speed: 292 knots (336 mph, 540 km/h)

Range: 2,050 nmi (2,360 mi, 3,800 km)

Service ceiling: 33,000 ft (10,060 m) empty; 23,000 ft (7,077 m) with 42,000 lb (19,090 kg) payload

Rate of climb: 1,830 ft/min (9.3 m/s)

Takeoff distance: 3,586 ft (1,093 m) at 155,000 lb (70,300 kg) max gross weight; 1,400 ft (427 m) at 80,000 lb (36,300 kg) gross weight[

Blackburn Buccaneer

General characteristics

Crew: 2 (pilot and observer)

Length: 63 ft 5 in (19.33 m)

Wingspan: 44 ft (13.41 m)

Height: 16 ft 3 in (4.97 m)

Wing area: 514.7 ft^2 (47.82 m^2)

Empty weight: 30,000 lb (14,000 kg)

Loaded weight: 62,000 lb (28,000 kg)

Powerplant: 2 × Rolls-Royce Spey Mk 101 turbofans, 11,100 lbf (49 kN) each

Performance
Maximum speed: 667 mph (580 knots, 1,074 km/h) at 200 ft (60 m)
Range: 2,300 mi (2,000 nmi, 3,700 km)
Service ceiling: 40,000 ft (12,200 m)
Wing loading: 120.5 lb/ft² (587.6 kg/m²)
Thrust/weight: 0.36

Armament
Guns: none
Hardpoints: 4 × under-wing pylon stations & 1× internal rotating bomb bay with a capacity of 12,000 lb (5,400 kg) and provisions to carry combinations of:
Rockets: 4 × Matra rocket pods with 18× SNEB 68 mm rockets each
Missiles: 2 × AIM-9 Sidewinders for self-defence, 2 × AS-30Ls *or* 2 × AS-37 Martel missiles *or* 2 × Sea Eagle missile
Bombs: Various unguided bombs, laser-guided bombs, as well as the Red Beard *or* WE.177 tactical nuclear bombs
Other: AN/ALQ-101 ECM protection pod, AN/AVQ-23 Pave SpikeLaser designator pod, Buddy refuelling pack *or* drop tanks for extended range/loitering time

Cessna 185 Spotter Aircraft
General characteristics
Crew: 1
Capacity: 5 passengers
Length: 25 ft 9 in (7.85 m)
Wingspan: 35 ft 10 in (10.92 m)
Height: 7 ft 9 in (2.36 m)
Wing area: 174 ft² (16.2 m²)
Empty weight: 1,748 lb (793 kg)
Gross weight: 3,350 lb (1,520 kg)
Powerplant: 1 × Continental IO-520-D , 300 hp (220 kW)
Propellers: 2-bladed constant speed, 6 ft 10 in (2.08 m) diameter

Performance
Maximum speed: 155 knots (178 mph; 287 km/h)
Cruise speed: 145 knots (167 mph; 269 km/h)
Stall speed: 49 knots (56 mph; 91 km/h)
Range: 720 nmi (830 mi; 1,330 km)
Service ceiling: 17,150 ft (5,230 m)
Rate of climb: 1,010 ft/min (5.1 m/s)

English Electric Canberra Bomber
General characteristics
Crew: 3
Length: 65 ft 6 in (19.96 m)
Wingspan: 64 ft 0 in (19.51 m)
Height: 15 ft 8 in (4.77 m)
Wing area: 960 ft² (89.19 m²)
Empty weight: 21,650 lb (9,820 kg)
Loaded weight: 46,000 lb (20,865 kg)
Max takeoff weight: 55,000 lb (24,948 kg)
Powerplant: 2 × Rolls-Royce Avon R.A.7 Mk.109 turbojets, 7,400 lbf (36 kN) each

Performance
Maximum speed: Mach 0.88 (580 mph, 933 km/h) at 40,000 ft (12,192 m)
Combat radius: 810 mi (700 nm, 1,300 km)
Ferry range: 3,380 mi (2,940 nm, 5,440 km)
Service ceiling: 48,000 ft (15,000 m)
Rate of climb: 3,400 ft/min (17 m/s)
Wing loading: 48 lb/ft² (234 kg/m²)
Thrust/weight: 0.32

Armament
Guns: 4 × 20 mm Hispano Mk V cannons mounted in rear bomb bay (500 rounds/gun), *or* 2 × 0.30 in (7.62 mm) machine gun pods
Rockets: 2 × unguided rocket pods with 37 × 2 in (51 mm) rockets, *or* 2 × Matra rocket pods with 18 × SNEB 68 mm rockets each
Missiles: A variety of missiles can be carried according to mission requirements, e.g: 2 × AS-30Lair-to-surface missiles

Bombs: Total of 8,000 lb (3,628 kg) of payload can be mounted inside the internal bomb bay and on two underwing hardpoints, with the ability to carry a variety of bombs. Typically, the internal bomb bay can hold up to 9 × 500 lb (227 kg) bombs, *or* 6 × 1,000 lb (454 kg) bombs, *or* 1× 4,000 lb (1,814 kg) bomb; while the pylons can hold 4 × 500 lb (227 kg) bombs, *or* 2 × 1,000 lb (454 kg) bombs.

Dassault Mirage III Fighter Aircraft

General characteristics

Crew: 1
Length: 15 m (49 ft 3.5 in)
Wingspan: 8.22 m (26 ft 11 in)
Height: 4.5 m (14 ft 9 in)
Wing area: 34.85 m^2 (375 ft^2)
Empty weight: 7,050 kg (15,600 lb)
Max takeoff weight: 13,500 kg (29,700 lb)
Powerplant: × SNECMA Atar 09C turbojet

Performance

Maximum speed: Mach 2.2 (2,350 km/h, 1,460 mph)
Range: 2,400 km (1,300 nm, 1,500 mi)
Service ceiling: 17,000 m (56,000 ft)
Rate of climb: 83.3 m/s (16,400 ft/min)
Wing loading: 387 kg/m^2 (79 lb/ft^2)

Armament

Guns: 2 × 30 mm (1.18 in) DEFA 552 cannons with 125 rounds per gun
Rockets: 2 × Matra JL-100 drop tank/rocket pack, each with 19 × SNEB 68 mm rockets and 66 US gallons (250 l) of fuel
Missiles: 2 × AIM-9 Sidewinders *or* Matra R550 Magics + 1 × Matra R530, 2 × AM-39 Exocetanti-ship missiles
Bombs: 4,000 kg (8,800 lb) of payload on 5 external hardpoints, including a variety of bombs, reconnaissance pods or drop tanks

Douglas C-54 Skymaster (Electronic Warfare Platform)

General characteristics

Crew: 4
Capacity: 50 troops
Length: 93 ft 10 in (28.6 m)
Wingspan: 117 ft 6 in (35.8 m)
Height: 27 ft 6 in (8.38 m)
Wing area: 1,460 ft^2 (136 m^2)
Empty weight: 38,930 lb (17,660 kg)
Loaded weight: 62,000 lb (28,000 kg)
Max takeoff weight: 73,000 lb (33,000 kg)
Powerplant: 4 × Pratt & Whitney R-2000-9 radial engines, 1,450 hp (1,080 kW) each

Performance

Maximum speed: 275 mph (239 knots, 442 km/h)
Cruise speed: 190 mph (165 knots, 310 km/h)
Range: 4,000 mi (6,400 km)
Service ceiling: 22,300 ft (6,800 m)
Wing loading: 42.5 lb/ft^2 (207 kg/m^2)
Power/mass: 0.094 hp/lb (160 W/kg)

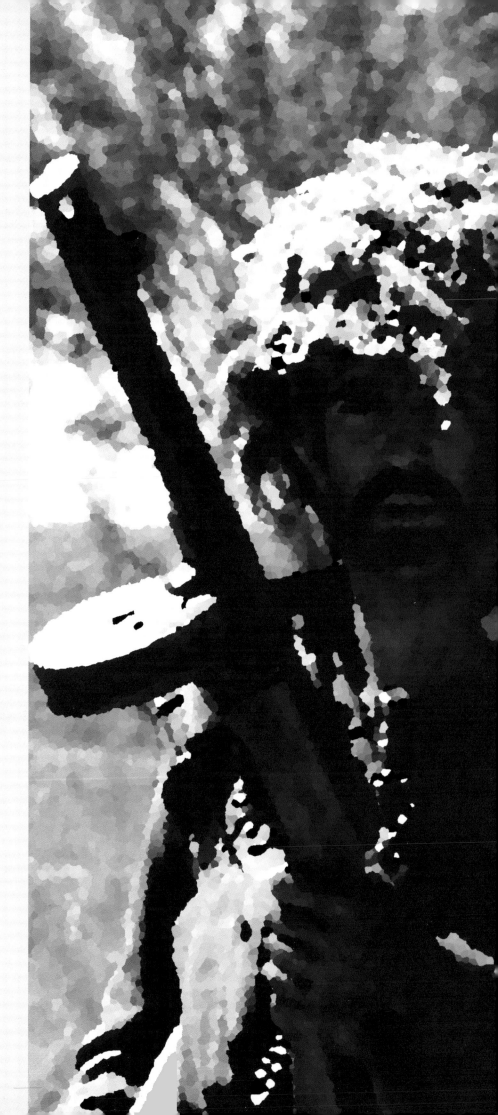

This book is dedicated to my beautiful wife of 30 years, Frances, who possesses all the virtues in abundance, with patience leading the charge.

My heartfelt thanks to my brother Jeremy, whose assistance with the English language was essential in making this book both readable as well as understandable.

Any errors are mine alone and apologies to my comrades from the Battle for Cassinga are hereby extended if they are misquoted, misrepresented or named in error.

Jan Volschenk, the soldier's notebook you found and preserved is invaluable proof that Cassinga was the SWAPO/PLAN regional headquarters and training base for its soldiers and not the refugee camp they told the world it was.

To my friend Helmut Labitzke who arranged for the translation of a section in the SWAPO/PLAN soldier's notebook from Oshiwambo into English—thanks Lappies; many promised but you delivered.

Lastly, my thanks to Colonel Jan Breytenbach who got us in and out of Cassinga with a minimum of casualties and largely intact, despite the difficulties thrust upon him by circumstances beyond the range of even his formidable planning capacity.

Mike McWilliams was born in 1951. He was conscripted into the South African Defence Force as an infantryman and immediately volunteered to join 1 Parachute Battalion, qualifying as a rifleman paratrooper in 1970. He served in 1, 2 and 3 Parachute Battalions until his last operation in 1978, the Battle For Cassinga. He has worked as a television cameraman for Rhodesian Television and the University of the Witwatersrand in South Africa. McWilliams is a championship skydiver and captained the Springbok team at the World Relative Work Championships in 1983, where his team won the Bronze Medal. He also captained the National Canopy Relative Work Team, winning the Deutschland Cup in 1982.